# Essays and Studies 2019

Series Editor: Elaine Treharne

# The English Association

The English Association is a membership body for individuals and organisations passionate about the English language and its literatures. Our membership includes teachers, students, authors, and readers, and is made up of people and institutions from around the world.

Our aim is to further the knowledge, understanding and enjoyment of English studies, and to foster good practice in their teaching and learning at all levels, by

- encouraging the study of English language and literature in the community at large
- working toward a fuller recognition of English as core to education
- fostering discussion about methods of teaching English at all levels
- supporting conferences, lectures, and publications
- responding to national consultations and policy decisions about the subject

More information about the Association is on our website: http://bit.ly/join-the-EA

# Publications

*The Year's Work in English Studies* - published annually, *The Year's Work in English Studies* is a qualitative narrative bibliographical review of scholarly work that year about the English language or literatures in English, from Old English to contemporary criticism.

*The Year's Work in Critical and Cultural Theory* - a companion volume in the field of critical and cultural theory, recording significant debates in a broad field of research in the humanities and social sciences.

*Essays and Studies* - published since 1910, *Essays and Studies* is an annual collection of essays on topical issues in English, edited by a different distinguished academic each year. The volumes cover a range of subjects and authors, from medieval to modern.

*English* - published quarterly, *English* is a forum for people who think hard and passionately about literature and who want to communicate those thoughts to a wide audience. It includes scholarly essays and reviews on all periods of literary history, and new work by contemporary poets.

*English 4 to 11* – published three times a year, this magazine contains material produced by, and for, the classroom leader. It is a reader-friendly magazine, backed by sound pedagogy, offering ideas for developing classroom practice.

*The Use of English* – published three times per year, this journal's articles and reviews are designed to encourage teachers to further their own interest and expertise in the subject.

*Newsletter* - produced three times per year, the *Newsletter* contains topical articles, news items, and interviews about English studies, and updates about The English Association's activities.

## *Benefits of Membership*

**Unity and voice** – members join others with a wealth of experience, knowledge, and passion for English, to foster the discussion of teaching methods and respond to national issues.

**Resources** – members can access high quality resources on the Association's website, and in its volumes, journals, magazines, and newsletters.

**Networking** – members can network with colleagues and leading practitioners, including joining national special interest groups and their local Regional Group. Members also are given reduced rates for the Association's conferences and other events.

Essays and Studies 2019

# Slow Scholarship: Medieval Research and the Neoliberal University

Edited by
**Catherine E. Karkov**

**for the English Association**

D. S. BREWER

ESSAYS AND STUDIES 2019
IS VOLUME SEVENTY-TWO IN THE NEW SERIES
OF ESSAYS AND STUDIES COLLECTED ON BEHALF OF
THE ENGLISH ASSOCIATION
ISSN 0071-1357

First published 2019
D. S. Brewer, Cambridge


D. S. Brewer is an imprint of Boydell & Brewer Ltd
PO Box 9, Woodbridge, Suffolk IP12 3DF, UK
and of Boydell & Brewer Inc.
668 Mt Hope Avenue, Rochester, NY 14620–2731, USA
website: www.boydellandbrewer.com


ISBN 978-1-84384-538-6

A CIP catalogue record for this book is available
from the British Library


The publisher has no responsibility for the continued existence or accuracy of
URLs for external or third-party internet websites referred to in this book, and
does not guarantee that any content on such websites is, or will remain, accurate
or appropriate


This publication is printed on acid-free paper

Printed and bound in Great Britain by
TJ International Ltd, Padstow, Cornwall

# Contents

# Illustrations

# Notes on Contributors

**Lara Eggleton** is a writer, historian, editor and arts consultant based in Leeds, UK. She is Managing Editor at Corridor8, a contemporary art and writing platform for the North of England, and a contributing writer for *Art Monthly, The Double Negative, a-n, Doggerland, Axisweb* and *this is tomorrow*, as well as numerous academic journals. She holds a PhD in Art History from the University of Leeds and is a visiting lecturer in Islamic Art and Orientalism at the University of Manchester and a tutor at Open College of the Arts. In her work she considers art across time and cultural spaces, which manifests in co-written publications and curatorial projects such as Medieval helpdesk.

**Karen Louise Jolly** is Professor of Medieval European History at the University of Hawaiʻi at Mānoa, where she also teaches pre-modern world history. Her research interests include popular religion, bilingual manuscripts and tenth-century Northumbria. She is currently working on a historical fiction project based on her study of Aldred in *The Community of St. Cuthbert in the Late Tenth Century: The Chester-le-Street Additions to Durham Cathedral Library A.IV.19* (2012).

**Chris Jones** is Professor of English at St Andrews University and a Fellow of the English Association. He is the author of *Strange Likeness: The Use of Old English in Twentieth-century Poetry* (2006), and *Fossil Poetry: Anglo-Saxon and Linguistic Nativism in Nineteenth-century Poetry* (2018). He was nearly in the first episode of the Great British Bake Off.

**Catherine E. Karkov** is Chair of Art History at the University of Leeds and a Fellow of the English Association and the Society of Antiquaries. She is the author of *The Art of Anglo-Saxon England* (2011) and the forthcoming *Imagining Anglo-Saxon England: Utopia, Heterotopia, Dystopia*. She is currently working on two projects focused on reimagining medieval studies.

**James Paz** is Lecturer in Early Medieval English Literature at the University of Manchester. He is the author of *Nonhuman Voices in Anglo-Saxon Literature and Material Culture* (2017) and the co-editor of *Medieval Science Fiction* (2016). His work has also appeared in *Exemplaria, New Medieval Literatures* and the *Journal of Medieval and Early Modern Studies*. His current research examines modern translations and poetic responses to Old English riddles, and he is also working on a long-term study of *cræft* in Anglo-Saxon literature.

**Andrew Prescott** is Professor of Digital Humanities at the University of Glasgow. He trained as a medieval historian at Westfield College and Bedford College in the University of London, where he completed a thesis on the Peasants' Revolt of 1381. He was from 1979 to 2000 a Curator of Manuscripts in the British Library, where he was involved in some of the Library's first digitisation projects, including *Electronic Beowulf*. He was Director of the Centre for Research into Freemasonry at the University of Sheffield from 2000 to 2007. He has also worked at the University of Wales Lampeter and King's College London. From 2012 to 2018, Andrew was Theme Leader Fellow for the Arts and Humanities Research Council strategic theme of 'Digital Transformations'. Andrew is a Fellow of the Society of Antiquaries and Fellow of the Royal Historical Society. His many publications include *English Historical Documents* (1988), *Towards the Digital Library* (1998), *The British Inheritance* (2000), *The Benedictional of St Æthelwold: A Masterpiece of Anglo-Saxon Art* (2002), *Marking Well* (2006) and *London and the Kingdom* (2008), as well as articles on the 1381 revolt, the history of the British Library's collections and the history of Freemasonry.

**Heather Pulliam** is a senior lecturer in the history of art at the University of Edinburgh. Her research focuses on the intersection between the marginal, experiential and material aspects of early medieval objects: for example, 'The Performative Cross: Blood, Water and Stone' considers the visual effects of rainfall on monumental sculpture; her monograph *Word and Image in the Book of Kells* explores how marginal creatures direct the reader's gaze; and 'Art and Avatar: Identity and Gesture in a Virtual World' analyses the intimate relationship engendered by the shape and scale of the Lewis chessmen. Heather was part of the curatorial team for *Celts: Art and Identity* at the British Museum/National Museum of Scotland (2015–16) and was awarded a Leverhulme Fellowship, *From 2D to 4D: Ireland's Medieval Crosses in Time, Motion and Environment* (2018–19).

# *Abbreviations*

| | |
|---|---|
| ASMMF | Anglo-Saxon Manuscripts in Microfiche Facsimile |
| CCSL | Corpus Christianorum Series Latina |
| CIDRAL | Centre for Interdisciplinary Research in Arts and Languages |
| CT | Computed Tomography |
| EETS | Early English Text Society |
| ESTC | English Short Title Catalogue |
| fols | folios |
| IFLA | International Federation of Library Associations and Institutions |
| IIIF | International Image Interoperability Framework |
| JISC | Joint Information Systems Committee |
| KPI | Key Performance Indicators |
| MOOC | Massive Open Online Course |
| MS | manuscript |
| NPR | National Public Radio |
| o. s. | original series |
| *PMLA* | *Proceedings of the Modern Language Association* |
| REF | Research Excellence Framework |
| RTI | Reflectance Transformation Imaging |
| *THE* | *Times Higher Education* |

Slow Collaborations

# Introduction: A Slow and Ongoing Collaboration

## CATHERINE E. KARKOV

Born and nurtured under the sign of Industrialization ... [the 20th century] ... first invented the machine and then modelled its lifestyle after it. Speed became our shackles. We fell prey to the same virus: 'the fast life' that fractures our customs and assails us even in our homes. ... Against those who confuse efficiency with frenzy, we propose the vaccine of an adequate portion of sensual gourmandise pleasure, to be taken with slow and prolonged enjoyment. ... Real culture is here to be found.[1]

Those words are from the 'Slow Food Manifesto' released as something of an artistic performance on 10 December 1989. The manifesto is, of course, a document about the preparation and experience of food, but its words are equally applicable to the preparation and experience of scholarship, perhaps especially scholarship that deals with sensual objects, with art, whether visual or literary – and by scholarship I mean both teaching and research, as well as the thinking and practices that surround them. As has been the case with food, our scholarship has become shackled to speed and profitability. Several years ago, Isabelle Stengers pointed out that the idea that we are primarily researchers rather than scholars 'comes from the laboratory sciences, but today that has redefined everything else ... the cost has been steep and has created a vulnerability that is now being brought to light'.[2] As Stengers suggested, we now look to practices rather than universities.

This book has been a slow collaboration. It began as a series of papers on 'Slow Scholarship in the Digital Age', delivered at the Leeds International Medieval Congress in 2014. Our intention was that a book

---

[1]   http://slowfoodaustralia.com.au/about-us/manifesto/; see also http://www.slowfood.com (both accessed 27 March 2017).
[2]   Isabelle Stengers quoted in Erik Bordeleau, 'The Care of the Possible: Isabelle Stengers interviewd by Erik Bordeleau', *Scapegoat: Architecture/Landscape/Political Economy* 1 (2011), 12–27, at 12.

should follow quickly, that this was a timely topic, but the ever-increasing demands of academic life and/or the demands of establishing a life outside of academia took their toll. The essays were left to age and mature. They were rethought, revised, tasted and tested like slowly cooked stews; some new ingredients were added, and others omitted from the final drafts. The digital has become less of a focus in some instances and more of a focus in others. The IMC sessions were inspired in part by the increasing demands from our universities for digital archives of our publications and research activities, for open access publications, for MOOCs, and for the use of 'blended learning', which in some instances seemed to mean simply using digital resources, blogs and/or assignments that needed to be completed online. Why should such practices be promoted as 'best practice' for all when they might add nothing of value to the way research is presented or subjects taught, and might add nothing to a student's interest in or engagement with our material? We are not anti-digital, as several of the essays that follow make clear, but the digital needs slow thinking. Digital resources and virtual environments are no substitute for working with the things, books, monuments and places we study and teach, nor are they a substitute for encounters with place, being in place and being with and in community. The digital can often serve only to isolate and separate us. Online discussions are not a replacement for personal interaction with fellow students and scholars. They cannot replicate, nor should they try to, the intimacy, rhythm, space and immediacy of face-to-face discussion and debate.[3] They can have a negative impact on concentration, close reading or looking and personal responsibility. The virtual at its worst is a place of isolation, anonymity, surveillance and violence. It can also leave us feeling exhausted. Sometimes we just need to disconnect.

The second, and related impetus for the collection came in part from the UK's 2014 REF (Research Excellence Framework) exercise, a subject that will reappear in several of the essays that follow. REF demands speed and takes up increasing amounts of our time. In 2014 established scholars were expected to have four preferably 'world-leading' publications written and in the public domain by the exercise's cut-off date of 31 December 2013. As soon as one exercise is completed preparation for the next one begins. Even if a department or university does well, much time is spent on determining where we got it wrong, and where and how we might be

---

[3]    See, for example, Richard Sennett, *The Craftsman* (Harmondsworth: Penguin, 2009); Nicholas Carr, *The Shallows: How the Internet is changing the way we think, read and remember* (London: Atlantic Books, 2011); Julie Hobsbawm, *Fully Connected: Surviving and thriving in an age of overload* (London: Bloomsbury, 2017).

able to improve our scores in future. Of course, all of this activity takes time away from the activities on which we ought to be focusing: teaching and research. Reading groups are formed and we hurriedly read through our colleagues' work (published or unpublished), advise, critique and score – and I say this is done hurriedly not because we don't care, but because we simply lack the time to do it otherwise. (A recent study estimates that academics now work 55 hours a week on top of any time they might wish to devote to research.[4]) External readers are often brought in to contribute their expertise. For purposes of REF we must beware of saying the same thing, or publishing 'yet again' on the same subject, of revisiting or revising or contradicting something we have said in an earlier publication. Collaboration, co-authoring or co-editing can be problematic, as we must be able to clearly distinguish our work from that of our collaborators for the REF panel, and collaborating with a colleague whose work will be assessed by the same panel means that the publication will count for only one of you. Above all, each publication should be world-leading (4*), or failing that at least internationally excellent (3*), as these are the only scores that bring in the (ever decreasing) government funding. All of this is meant to prove to the government and taxpayers that universities and scholarship are worth supporting, that they provide value for money, that they make a contribution to the nation and the nation's standing in the world – especially a financial contribution. It replaces the university's duty to demonstrate its responsibility to society with the university's ability to demonstrate that it is 'spending money responsibly'.[5] As is frequently pointed out, the vast sums of money spent on REF would be much better spent on funding students and actual research.[6]

REF is also a tool of the neoliberal corporate university. It keeps us busy producing 'outputs', creating 'impact', bringing in profit in the form of research grants or spin-off companies. REF is a UK problem, but the corporate ideology and structure, and the way in which it forces scholars to be complicit in maintaining both are, if not universal problems, all but universal problems. Slow scholarship offers a means of resisting and

---

[4] David Matthews, 'If You Love Research Academia may not be for You', *Times Higher Education* (*THE*), 8 November 2018: https://www.timeshigh-ereducation.com/blog/if-you-love-research-academia-may-not-be-you?fb-clid=IwAR1FRfvdWtWiP851H3eRphu3hrBlrABzvDM60X_ePZ9cB6qwp6p_XhZGR1U#survey-answer (accessed 23 November 2018).
[5] Thomas Docherty, *Complicity: Criticism between collaboration and commit-ment* (London: Rowman & Littlefield, 2016), 37, 41.
[6] See especially, Derek Sayer, *Rank Hypocrisies: The insult of the REF* (London: SAGE Swifts, 2014).

fighting back, a means of saying no to the constant demands for more, for better, for newer and more elaborate ways of counting, or assessing or establishing accountability. It is a means first and foremost of reclaiming time, time to think, read, talk, collaborate about and around what is of value to scholars and scholarly communities, rather than university administrators, research council funding agendas or government committees. It is a means of experiencing time, place and the things we study differently. It is a means of taking back the time to do the research we want to do rather than that which our department or university management teams might urge us to do because it will bring in a bigger grant – and *funded* research is equated with *better* research.

Ironically, the overproduction of research demanded by exercises such as REF, or indeed the demands of hiring, promotion and tenure committees, threatens the quality, integrity and innovative nature of the research we do. It is easier and faster to produce articles and chapters on demand than it is to produce books but, as some publishers have noted, even books 'have fewer ideas and play it safe so as not to upset the status quo'.[7] It is only by upsetting the status quo, however, that we can create a space for change. Who determines that a paradigm-changing book that might take years or even decades to produce is of less value, less worthy of a scholar's time and attention, than four other shorter types of publication? Who determines how much is enough – enough articles written, enough research income generated, enough PhD students trained (but for what jobs)? We are continually told that we must improve, but to what end? And if improvement is always necessary, then we are by default always already not doing enough. A recent survey of university staff in the UK revealed that nearly 75 per cent were unhappy with the administration of their institutions, citing in particular lack of time to do the work they were asked to do, pressure to reach publication targets, and lack of support and respect from senior management.[8] Moreover, improvement in administrative terms means only improvement that can be counted or otherwise measured. Thinking cannot be counted, nor depth of thought measured.

---

[7]   Lindsay Waters, *Enemies of Promise: Publishing, perishing, and the eclipse of scholarship* (Chicago: University of Chicago Press, 2004), 35; Lawrence Busch, *Knowledge for Sale: The neoliberal takeover of higher education* (Cambridge, MA: MIT Press, 2017), 65–7.

[8]   Matthew Reisz, 'Overpaid and Overbearing: UK staff on management', *THE* 2,299 (30 March–5 April 2017), 6–7: https://www.timeshighereducation.com/news/overpaid-and-overbearing-uk-university-staff-management (accessed 23 November 2018).

On the other hand, if we are kept busy with the constant counting and assessing exercises, kept busy trying to achieve 'better' (and demonstrating how we are doing it), we will not have time to think, talk, meet, plot, upset the status quo and take back our power as scholars to shape university strategies and priorities, to create the universities in which we would really like to work. I am hardly the first to make these observations:[9] rather I, and the other contributors to this volume, wish to add our voices to the growing call for collaborative and collective action.

If we say nothing, we have for all intents and purposes accepted the idea that we do need to do more, and we do need to do it better and faster, and that scholarship is a product like any other that it can be assigned a monetary value and be bought and sold for a financial profit. Thomas Docherty has likened the situation in which we find ourselves now to that of the boiling frog scenario. If you drop a frog in boiling water it will leap out, but leave it in cool water and turn up the heat bit by bit, and it will remain still and allow itself to be boiled to death. Each little change in our freedom to conduct our research and scholarship in our own time and as we see fit, each small limit to our ability to have a voice in the strategies and priorities of our universities that we accept in silence signals our agreement and makes it increasingly difficult to bring about change of any sort.[10] We need to assume responsibility and demand that our institutions do the same. We need ethical universities and ethical scholarship, a reversal of the gradual changes that have brought us from an ethos of responsibility to one of accountability.[11]

---

[9]    See, for example, Maggie Berg and Barbara Seeber, *The Slow Professor: Challenging the culture of speed in the academy* (Toronto: University of Toronto Press, 2016); Wendy Brown, *Undoing the Demos: Neoliberalism's stealth revolution* (New York: Zone, 2015); Stefan Collini, *What are Universities For?* (Harmondsworth: Penguin, 2012); idem, *Speaking of Universities* (London: Verso, 2017); Thomas Doherty, *Universities at War* (London: SAGE Swifts, 2014); idem, *Complicity*; Susan Mountz et al., 'Slow Scholarship: A feminist politics of resistance through collective action in the neoliberal university', *ACME: an International E-Journal for Critical Geographies* 14.4 (2015), 1235–59; Bill Reading, *The University in Ruins* (Cambridge, MA: Harvard University Press, 1997); Sayer, *Rank Hypocrisies*; Busch, *Knowledge for Sale*. See also the 'Reclaiming Our University' manifesto written by staff at the University of Aberdeen: https://reclaimingouruniversity. wordpress.com (accessed 23 November 2018).

[10]    Docherty, *Complicity*, 22.

[11]    Docherty, *Complicity*, 27–50. For an interesting exploration of the ethics of scholarship, see Roland Betancourt, 'Beyond Foucault's Laugh: On the ethical practice of medieval art history', in *Postcolonising the Medieval Image*, ed. Eva Frojmovic and Catherine E. Karkov (New York: Routledge, 2017), 144–66.

The situation in which we now find ourselves has sometimes been likened to feudalism or colonialism, but it is better thought of as a situation of postcolonialism, and one calling for postcolonial strategies of response and resistance. We have been both oppressed and, in failing to resist, been more or less active participants in our own oppression. Docherty, as noted above, has been especially concerned with pointing out that our failure to resist makes us increasingly complicit in regularising and reinforcing the very institutional ideologies, values and practices we seek to critique and overturn.[12] In much the same vein, the organisers of the 2017 'Radicalism and the University' conference called for an exploration of the meaning and value of radicalism in today's university, in which the very idea of theorising or practicing "radical" history has become yet another marketing tool.[13] How can institutions that cooperate in the deportation of immigrant staff, the surveillance of overseas students and the employment of staff on zero-hour contracts justify their claim to teach and practise radical history and politics? And can radical scholarship be maintained in any meaningful way within such institutions?

More generally, we should be asking questions about the right of universities to own our research, a practice that seemingly also gives them the right to brand and market it as they choose. We need to slow down and take the time to examine the terms of our employment and the terms that seem increasingly to structure and define our scholarly activities: excellence, impact, efficiency, austerity, value for money, best practice, academic freedom, even scholarship.[14] The shifting uses and definitions of such terms, and the contexts in and by which they are used and defined, need to be identified and thought through slowly. We must each, in the words of the anonymous author of *The Order of the World* (as translated by James Paz) be 'the deep-minded one who lives with courage [we] must inquire into the shape of things'.[15]

***

[12]   Docherty, *Complicity*. See also Riyad A. Shajahan, 'From "no" to "yes": Postcolonial perspectives on resistance to neoliberal higher education', *Discourse: Studies in the Cultural Politics of Education* 35.2 (2014), 219–32.

[13]   CFP: Radicalism and the University (Colchester, 13–14 June 2017). In: *H-ArtHist*, 10 March 2017, https://arthist.net/archive/14930 (accessed 27 March 2017).

[14]   See further Collini, *Speaking of Universities*; Docherty, *Complicity*; Brown, *Undoing the Demos*; John Mowitt, 'The Searing of the University', *Kronos: The Journal of Southern African Histories* 43.1 (2017), 99–113. I am grateful to John Mowitt for sharing a copy of his paper with me prior to its publication.

[15]   See below p. 35.

The essays in this volume do not take radical action. They are slow and very personal responses to the scholarly culture of the present moment. In moments of crisis and threat people do turn to the arts and humanities for a way of understanding a situation, but also for pleasure, and even survival.[16] As arts and humanities scholars, our own work can offer a way of finding both hope and pleasure in yet another moment of crisis in our fields. The essays collected here detail ways in which we as individual scholars cope, ways in which we escape, ways in which we find time for ourselves and the work we want to do, and ways in which we must demand better. They each take time to find, explore, return to or reflect on the joy of scholarship, or the joy that brought us to scholarly research and careers in the first place. They find joy in taking the time to speak and listen to each other. While they might not address issues such as academic freedom directly, they have been written as declarations of the academic freedom that comes with slow thinking, slow reading, slow writing and slow looking. As such, they are statements of resistance against the incessant demands of contemporary academic life.

Collaborations cannot be forced. They take their own time to evolve. Some are planned, some are the result of chance or serendipitous encounters, but the most fertile ones are often those that are furthest from the business partnership models advocated by so many universities and research councils. Lara Eggleton's 'Research as Folly, or, How to Productively "Ruin" Your Research', reflects on her career as a younger scholar, moving from a PhD on the medieval Alhambra and nineteenth-century travel literature to a career in art writing and collaboration with contemporary artists. She identifies herself as a member of the precariat, those generally younger scholars working in multiple part-time positions that bring little, if any, job security, often little income, and often involve disproportionately heavy workloads. She has been in the position of so many young academics who find themselves exploited by university systems and priorities, working as adjuncts often on zero-hour and/or teaching only contracts. Her essay documents her partnership in multiple collaborations that have evolved owing to the precarious employment circumstances in which a younger scholar found herself, revealing the ways in which decisions, dialogues, interests and partnerships, took their time to develop organically within their own unique set of circumstances and environments.

[16] See especially Irina Dumitrescu, ed., *Rumba under Fire: The arts of survival from West Point to Delhi* (New York: Punctum Books, 2016).

The medieval, Eggleton notes, offers a mirror to her own scholarly evolution. The Alhambra has always been hard to pin down. It is not one monument but many, and it has been and can still be encountered in many different ways by its inhabitants, architects, artists, scholars and by travellers over the centuries. It had a long, slow diversity of becoming. The Alhambra is a ruin, and Eggleton embraces the monument with its slow weathering and decay, its rebuilding and restoration, and its place in the environment as a metaphor for her own slow scholarship. Ruins, failures and follies give birth to new forms, ideas and opportunities. Because of her precarious university employment, she slowed down and took the time to think about the work she enjoyed doing, the work she wanted to do, and the way she found to do it. Her collaborations with visual artists, writers and communities are still dependent on temporary contracts and changing circumstances, but they also give her freedom from the accountability, assessment, targets, quotas, research and impact agendas of life in the neoliberal university. She has found the time to let her ideas evolve and change, to discard a path of research if it becomes unproductive, following, as she puts it, the 'natural rhythm of our influences'. Like the ruin, her scholarship has gradually been shaped by and become one with her environment.

Like a number of the contributors to the volume, Eggleton has found inspiration in interlacing ideas and objects from different time periods with each other, and this has led her to become increasingly aware of and interested in the importance of experiencing objects, monuments and places. The things we study sometimes have secret lives, and so do the scholars that study them. She has become a traveller, encountering things and places across time and space, exploring different aspects of embodied understanding and the encounter of humans and things across cultures. Rather than specialising, she has diversified, and through her multiple collaborations, slogging, research and exhibitions, has retained – or perhaps returned to – joy and freedom in her research and writing.

A single word can have different meanings, valances, memories and pronunciations. Words need to be spoken, written and read with care. They need to be thought over, chewed over, digested and woven together slowly, with deep thought, as the two essays in the *Slow Words* section remind us. James Paz notes that English poetry began with eating words, slowly and carefully, with rumination, concentration and focus. As with the two essays in the section on collaboration, Paz explores the ways in which the past, in this case the practices of Anglo-Saxon poets, can inform his own contemporary practice as a scholar, editor and author. Anglo-Saxon poems were produced slowly. They might be passed on orally over many generations before ever being written down. When written, every word, every letter was written slowly, by hand, with quill and ink. Books came together slowly, moving over months or years from the skin of a living animal, to a collection of written texts, to an entire bound manuscript. The Anglo-Saxons celebrated book production and its time in their riddles (especially the famous Exeter Book Riddle 26, which survives in the same manuscript as the poem on which Paz concentrates here), and in their art, which from its earliest days is filled with books, readers, writers and the joy and mystery of letters and words. Anglo-Saxon art and poetry are full of patterns, interlacings and knots of images and words that, far from being 'mere' ornament, are meant to be puzzled over, untangled slowly, and designed to flow into or spiral through or across texts and surfaces, leaving a trail of repetition, metamorphosis and innuendo that it is up to the reader/viewer to follow and connect. They demand to be encountered slowly. Translation is a process of getting to know a text slowly, and getting to know previous translations of that text just as slowly. Words and our understanding of them change over time, things get lost over time, texts age and ripen over time.

Paz's translation of the enigmatic poem sometimes known as *The Order of the World* takes place slowly, in his own time, for his own interests in the past and practice in the present. It is not a means of resistance so much as a means of creating a space of intimacy with his sources, albeit one that remains stubbornly outside the demands and pace of exercises such as REF. As he says, the larger project of which this translation is a part may not be completed for another decade or two. As the poem he returns to each morning asks him to do, he listens, hears, witnesses and learns.

Chris Jones reads the poem *The Grave* slowly, line by line and word by word, allowing the poem to build its imagery and its meaning gradually. Poems are after all built slowly and carefully, like houses. This is also a very personal reading of the poem, one that he interlaces with some of the events of his own life, and this leads him to suggest a new school of reading: Personalism. Personalism is embodied reading, emotional reading, a practice that is every bit as important and vital – perhaps more vital – as historicism. This is exactly the type of originality that, with its combination of scholarship and/as practice, more often than not goes unrewarded in exercises such as REF. It does not sit well within assigned research or disciplinary classifications. Nevertheless, his work leads Jones to a relineation of *The Grave* that frees it from its bonds of binary pairs, its traditional classifications, fills what had been seen as the problematic holes in its structure and meaning, and offers us a new and important way of reading Old English poetry.

*Slow Looking.* Things are arguably much slower than words because things move slowly, if they move at all. Things have long biographies. Some things remain in place, changing and decaying gradually over the centuries, like the ruins that Lara Eggleton takes as her inspiration. Other things travel over distances – shorter or longer – sometimes changing form, adjusting (or not) to each new environment as they go. Or they move from collection to collection, becoming more or less accessible depending on institutional policies. They, like words, have agency, but they also have a stubborn materiality that cannot be replicated, and that unfolds itself slowly over time, creating ghosts and doppelgangers as the centuries pass by. Heather Pulliam's 'Rethinking Slow Looking: Encounters with Clonmacnoise' turns to the concern for slow looking that has become more and more a focus of art historical research and teaching over the past five years or so. Exercises in slow looking are certainly essential but, as Pulliam points out, we sometimes too easily assume that we are caught up in a series of binaries, fast vs slow, presence vs absence, original vs surrogate, and this can be limiting. Classifications are confining. Her essay grows out of her ongoing research project on the Irish high crosses, and specifically the ninth- to tenth-century group of crosses at the monastery of Clonmacnoise in County Offaly, and the casts that have been made of them. She thinks about the monuments through the notion of transformation of the monuments, of their environment and of the viewer. The original crosses have been moved inside the Visitors' Centre, which transforms their appearance and materiality completely, and replicas have been erected in their original positions among the monastic buildings. Additionally, digital scans have been made of the crosses. Together the originals and their copies allow for a transformed viewing experience. Moving the monuments inside allows for their study slowly and without the worry of changing weather or lighting conditions. The copies fix details, facilitating a very different, 2D in the case of the digital scans, study of their imagery and inscriptions.

Throughout history though, changing weather would have transformed the way the monuments looked and were experienced, and the concrete replicas still allow visitors to experience these changes – if they take the time to do so. Pulliam has visited the site many times and continues to do so. She has documented the way rain falls on the crosses, and how one can shelter beneath the cross-arm of the Cross of the Scriptures. She has experienced how different emotional states or numbers of other visitors change the way she thinks about the crosses. Centring in on the single carving of the Hand of God on the underside of the southern arm of the Cross of the Scriptures, she demonstrates the need for a viewer to move slowly around the cross, looking at it from different distances and vantage points, and thinking about it always from the perspective of an embodied viewer (Personalism!), in order to understand the multiple ways in which it creates meaning.

The difficult, fabulous and sometimes imaginary biography of the eighth-century Ruthwell Cross is the subject of my own chapter in the volume. The stone from which the cross is carved was millions of years in the making. It is sandstone, the product of the ebb and flow of water, of sedimentation, of volcanic activity deep beneath the earth pushing it upwards towards the air. It is elemental, but scholars rarely take the time to encounter it that way. It is also fragile, fragmented, broken, decaying and dying. It has a long slow life-cycle that needs to be thought through slowly and merits encounter through the elements from and by which the monument was forged. Its materials and materiality cannot be replicated – one needs to spend time with the real thing.

The cross is also the product of human hands. Hands selected and carved these stones, felt the grains of quartz and other minerals of which they are composed. Hands also pulled down the monument, smashed it and buried parts of it. We can still touch the stone as did those centuries of hands, feel its warmth or cold, the lines of its cracks and fractures – though this is, of course, discouraged and made especially difficult now that the monument is safely confined within its pit rather than rising up from the earth and grass that originally supported it. It took a long time to carve the cross. It is well crafted, both in its carving and in its visual and theological composition. We should not overlook or dismiss any of its details no matter how long it takes us to think about how and why they might be important. We need to take the time to understand what it is we're looking at and what questions we want to ask of it. Meanings spiral outward from the monument forwards and backwards through time. Its deep past is haunted by more recent events, and what it once was is not what it is today. Things have become lost over time. Thinking about the cross in this way is enjoyable and leads to unexpected synergies and connections over time, but it does not necessarily reach the 4* level of research demanded by university peer review panels, and it certainly doesn't bring in any income through either grant 'capture' or impact activities. Thinking about the cross in this way is something I must find the time to do in my own time.

*Slow Manuscripts*. Karen Jolly's transcription of the Durham Collectar, and concomitant study of Aldred's glosses to it, is also slow work, letter by letter work, as the title of her chapter makes clear, work that requires deep thought. All transcriptions and editions of medieval texts require us to deal with handwriting, but in her work Jolly has become focused on the hand. How did the hands of the scribes who glossed this manuscript work – especially Aldred's? How did hand, eye and brain work together to form these letters? How do her hand, eye and brain work together now as she both transcribes them and attempts to imitate their forms? What will be lost to us if, in this digital age, we lose handwriting? (A question dear to my own heart as I write the draft of this introduction slowly on paper with fountain pen.) Earlier generations of scholars, editors and transcribers who worked with pen or pencil on paper still haunt the archive. It is essential for scholars to work with the original manuscript and with printed manuscript facsimiles in order to fully grasp the manuscript and its history but, as Jolly notes, digital tools are also essential to modern scholarship. They make texts and archives faster and easier to search, allow increased access to the things we study and new ways of engaging our students with the medieval past and scholarship on it. Close reading, close attention to things, be they texts or works of art, can be thoughtfully combined in the digital world to bring new synergies and excitement to our research and our teaching, and she offers some useful examples of how she does just that.

Slow thinking about Aldred and the Durham Collectar has brought Jolly to a new pleasure in novel writing. Her deep reading and transcription of Aldred's text has become interwoven with the imaginary world of the novel she is writing about him. Aldred did not write in isolation, but how did he work? What was the scriptorium like? What conversations, learning, chance encounters took place there? What landscapes did Aldred travel through? What views might he have looked out on while he worked? And what was his monastic community like? Manuscript production was communal work, as is scholarship on it today, and as are the strategies of resistance embraced by slow scholarship. Again, words matter, and we need the time to ponder their meanings and valences. We need to pay attention to words, not only in medieval texts, but also in the language through which scholarship and teaching are marketed and sold, the words used to describe or establish their relevance or value. We need to take the time to determine whether the questions we are asking are the ones that need to be asked, the ones that most matter to us or, as Jolly puts it, to the human condition rather than the market.

The relationship between the manuscript and its copying in different media is also at the heart of the volume's final essay, Andrew Prescott's 'Slow Digitisation and the Battle of the Books'. Prescott is especially concerned with and about the digitisation process, exploring some of the problems created by the rush to digitise, and some of the practices that could be adopted to ensure digital resources are accessible, useful and of sufficient quality for the work that is required of them. In a lecture delivered in 1993 Robin Alston, Professor of Library and Information Studies at University College London, voiced his concerns about the effects on libraries and archives of commercial interests and the creation of hypermarkets for information, a situation that Prescott shows has continued to worsen. The pressure on institutions to reach KPI (Key Performance Indicators) or 'widening participation' targets alone can lead to digitisation for nothing more than digitisation's own sake, resulting in poor-quality imaging, problems of functionality and erroneous information. Moreover, the number of hits a digital manuscript or archive receives is not an indicator of widening participation, increased knowledge exchange, or increased use by scholars, engagement with the material or access generally. It is an indicator of number of visits to a page (some perhaps accidental) and not of time spent with an image or manuscript.

The move to use commercial firms to undertake imaging has done nothing but add to existing problems. Imaging results can vary enormously, often being undertaken with no consideration of what users might want from an image, and archives or manuscripts can become *less* accessible, sometimes requiring hefty subscription fees for their use, and/or payments for top-quality images (always an issue for art historians). Prescott surveys a number of examples of both good and bad practice, several of which concern the digitisation of the *Beowulf* manuscript, whose anonymous scribes have attracted as much if not more attention than the famous Aldred. Kevin Kiernan's ground-breaking *Electronic Beowulf* is an example of the slow digital method. Its production was painstakingly slow, including imaging under ultra-violet, backlighting of text and continuous foregrounding of the needs of the scholars who would be consulting the manuscript, especially the need to bring out text that was hidden owing to damage. By contrast, the high-resolution images now available on the British Library's website allow none of that detail to be seen, but are the ones that most students and many (perhaps most) scholars will turn to now for study and publication of the manuscript, despite the fact that one can see even less in some images than one can in Kemp Malone's 1963 black-and-white print facsimile.

Prescott establishes digitisation as a toolbox. Digital facsimiles and archives need to be built slowly and with due consideration for such things as quality, hidden text or images, accessibility, and for the sorts of information that viewers will want from them. Slow digitisation is necessary to properly excavate the layers of a manuscript, and we must undertake the process under the guiding assumption that there is always something new to discover in a manuscript.

\*\*\*

There are a number of threads that unite the seven chapters of this volume: ecology, environment, concern for the humanities, resistance, evolution, experience and experiencing, the passage of time, the personal. All of these can be woven or knotted together in an overriding concern for and with place. We are each concerned in one way or another with the place(s) of scholarship, with our place(s) as scholars, with the places in which knowledge happens, with the places of the works we study and with the need to experience those works in the places in which they survive or were made, with the places in which we research and teach, and with the place of our scholarship, of the institutions and practices on which it depends, and of the university in the wider world. And all these places are places of community, communities of the past and of the present and communities that grow and develop in the space between the two. We all work as members of these communities, and we all share a concern for their future. We offer these essays out of our concern, and our belief that we need to act together to bring about change. These are essays we wanted to write, not ones that needed to be written for administrative exercises or tenure and promotion files. Although they deal with some very different subjects, they resonate with and echo each other in exciting ways. They create and maintain a dialogue that has extended outward to our individual and collective departments, universities, professional and social networks. This book is part of an effort to expand that dialogue further, to keep the conversation going.

# Research as Folly, or, How to Productively 'Ruin' Your Research

## LARA EGGLETON

In the months following my PhD viva, I struggled to decide what direction my research should take. Given the transhistorical and thematic nature of my thesis, a monograph seemed the wrong approach, so I set about the task of publishing it as a series of articles and book chapters.[1] I learned that the Alhambra, an Islamic fortress-palace turned Castilian residence, turned global tourist destination in Spain, is an historical object far too big for a single study, encompassing multiple material and immaterial histories. The very thing that had attracted me to the monument – its potential for blowing apart historical and disciplinary categories – is also what made it so difficult to contain in a single publication. My central assertion, that the Alhambra cannot be fully understood through a singular synchronic lens but must be viewed across and between its periods of transformation, led me to conclude that through its constant appropriation and reimagining it remained permanently displaced. Throughout my time studying this slippery and illusive subject, I dabbled in being a Medievalist, an Islamicist, a Mediterraneanist, a Renaissance/Early Modern scholar, a Victorianist and even a 'Medievalismist'. Having taken up the problem of ornament and decoration as intermediary categories elided by the Western canon, I also found myself at odds with my own field. 'Non-Western' art historians have made significant headway challenging the discipline's Eurocentrism in recent years, but progress is slow and methodological tools thin on the ground. My peripatetic and at times combative scholarly journey has resulted in a pluralistic and fragmented research profile, causing no small amount of anxiety about how to define my specialism and my work, often against the grain of job specifications and funding remits.

The benefit of this halting approach is that I have learned to see the value in slowing down, in pausing to consider the strengths and versatility

---

[1]    Lara Eve Eggleton (2011) 'Re-envisioning the Alhambra: Readings of architecture and ornament from medieval to modern', PhD thesis, University of Leeds. Available through White Rose Etheses Online: <http://etheses.whiterose.ac.uk/1736/> (accessed 9 February 2018).

of my research, in recalling the joy of writing, researching and teaching. I've become more discerning when using the term 'interdisciplinary' and developed a more carefully considered rationale for entering into particular collaborations. Rather than grabbing my nearest colleague and leaping through funding hoops, I've identified mutually productive links both in and outside academia. I've also pursued avenues for my writing that lie off the beaten publishing track, and that have allowed me to explore ideas responsively and creatively. The result is that my subsequent research and parallel projects have grown organically out of a need to let my ideas and interests take on a life of their own. This has convinced me that the secret to a healthy and nourishing career is allowing space for ideas to evolve (or devolve), in line with the natural rhythms of our influences, preoccupations and concerns. In this way, slow scholarship might be imagined as a kind of ruin; a structure that becomes naturally subsumed and integrated into its surroundings, embodying changes to the researcher and her chosen subjects or objects over time. It is a gradual becoming, with productive and destructive forces working together to create something new.

## Falling into Ruin

There has of late been much talk about ruins. The 2014 Tate Britain exhibition, *Ruin Lust*, attracted a surprising degree of attention (a lot of it negative)[2] – while conferences and university lecture series have favoured ruin-related themes. In a discussion with a friend about her recent trip to China, we observed the Western-centric fascination with ruins, compared with nations that seem to prefer historic monuments artificially returned to their imagined 'original' state. In contrast, British monuments are often restored to a particular stage of ruin, and a number of architectural follies of the Romantic period were actually conceived in this transitory, disintegrating image of the past. As potent symbols of the transience of civilisations and the human condition more generally, Brian Dillon (co-curator of *Ruin Lust*, with Emma Chambers and Amy Concannon) has remarked that among its many associations and evocations, the ruin can represent an 'ideal of beauty that is alluring exactly because of its flaws and failures', as well as symbolise 'a certain melancholic or maundering state of mind'.[3]

---

[2]    *Ruin Lust* was on at Tate Britain from 2 March to 18 May 2014. Some reviewers found it conceptually thin, e.g. Rosemary Hill writing in *London Review of Books* 36:7 (3 April 2014), 20.

[3]    Brian Dillon, *Ruin Lust: Artists' fascination with ruins, from Turner to the present day* (London: Tate Publishing, 2014), 5.

These evocations of imperfection and a drifting focus stand strongly in opposition to ideas of productivity, efficiency and progressivism that saturate our '24–7' postcapitalist work ethic. The implicit warning lies within so many working environments: to slow down or lose focus is to fail, to fall behind in the race.

I'm attracted to the metaphor of the ruin because it sees the natural processes of death and decay as giving rise to new forms and possibilities, under the right circumstances. It has resonance within literary, visual and material histories, not least of all because it imagines regeneration through disintegration. Tim Edensor, in his keynote address at a conference at the University of Manchester, 'Big Ruins', argued that any building or urban setting fallen into disrepair could be called a ruin, while heavily restored and maintained monuments, such as Rome's Coliseum, could not.[4] By this logic the agent of ruin might be interpreted as neglect, whereas Florence Hetzler has identified this naturally occurring 'ruin time' as having a unifying effect. She has defined ruins as 'the disjunctive product of the intrusion of nature upon the human-made *without* the loss of the unity of the original structure'.[5] In line with this, each ruin has a maturation time or a cycle of maturation times, which imagines it having a beginning, middle and end phase. Similarly, my research has gone through multiple transformations, with some layers receding and others emerging in response to various outside forces, which give it shape, form and detail.

One shaping factor is my apparent membership in what has been coined in sociological circles 'the precariat'. Dependent on part-time and temporary contracts, with little or no job security, the precarious worker is at risk of poverty and exploitation. At the same time, a more positive view sees workers such as myself as free-spirited and nonconformist, rejecting the norms of the old working class (steeped in stable labour), as well as those of bourgeois materialism.[6] While I'm not sure precisely where I stand on the freedom–exploitation spectrum, I can confidently state that work (the nature, amount and frequency of), and my particular relationship to it (my motivations for and attitudes towards it), are never far from my mind. At the very least, being part of the precariat makes

---

[4]    CIDRAL conference: 'Big Ruins: The aesthetics and politics of supersized decay', convened by Paul Dobraszczyk for the School of Arts, Languages and Cultures, 14 May 2014.

[5]    Florence M. Hetzler, 'Ruin Time and Ruins', *Leonardo* 21:1 (1988), 51–5, at 51.

[6]    Guy Standing, *The Precariat: The new dangerous class* (London & New York: Bloomsbury Academic, 2011), 9.

one value the time spent working, and not working (which represents its own kind of productivity), in a conscious and reflective way. I'm one of a growing precariat workforce of educated specialists who are able to ask the question: 'How does a life look when it doesn't define itself in relation to the status of wage labour, but rather through the desire to freely decide one's own conditions for living and working?'[7] These conditions, which in my case usually means less pay for work that I enjoy, also require me to redefine what it means to be a specialist. On the contrary, with the scarcity of permanent academic posts in my field, being a 'non-specialist', jumping nimbly from project to project, holds increased appeal.

In the face of austerity and waning support for the arts and humanities, it is arguably in my best interests to diversify my areas of knowledge. Rather than seeing this as a threat to my specialism, I recognised the potential for deepening and enriching aspects my research and expanding my methodological repertoire. Moreover, the benefits of doing independent research are clear: free of the fetters of impact agendas (with outputs and publication quotas imposed irrespective of discipline), it is possible to let my research pause, breathe and take in the view. In arts and humanities subjects it almost always pays off to nurture a project to maturity, rather than scrambling to produce an arbitrary number of 'REFable' publications. While part-time or sessional work lacks stability, it does allow the gradual accumulation of knowledge, experience and inspiration from a range of contexts. With a little patience and a healthy bit of distance, slow scholarship can result in more considered and refined, if less frequent, outputs.

## In and Out of Time

The ruin and its related schools of thought crept onto my radar at the exact point when I was grappling, like so many of us, with the temporal and cultural boundaries that restrict a deeper understanding of historical objects, texts or monuments. It was unrealistic for me to acquire the many languages and specialisms necessary to discuss the Alhambra across its many lives and afterlives. However, having time to contemplate and delve further into different periods opened up a space to consider recurring themes and problems, such as the politics of reception, the dynamics

[7]    Marion von Osten, 'Irene ist Viele! Or What We Call "Productive Forces"', *e-flux journal – Are You Working Too Much? Post Fordism, Precarity, and the Labor of Art* (Berlin: Sternberg Press, 2011), 42.

of difference, and the irreducibility of style to singular cultural identities. Positioning different periods of production next to one another allowed their seemingly disparate elements to cross-pollinate, and less straight-forward or agreeable aspects of its material history to emerge. Through this slowed-down process I was able to properly attend to the objects that caused the most problems when I was trying to pull my thesis into a coherent whole, and to reconsider the categories, or lack thereof, which rendered them so problematic.

To give one example, it was only during my viva and subsequent corrections that I discovered the 'secret life' of a large marble chimney-piece that now occupies an upper room of the Palace of Charles V on the Alhambra grounds. Closer study revealed the transformation of a commissioned Italian Renaissance fireplace into an unusual altarpiece in the fifteenth century, used in a royal chapel that had served as a council chamber under the Nasrid kings.[8] Its integration into the Islamic deco-rative programme was only discovered and reversed in the 1930s, and its unusual history attests to a stylistic crisis at two distinctive points in history. Taking a cue from Alexander Nagel and Christopher Wood, I argued that this might be seen as an example of 'citation' through the reuse of art objects, what they describe as 'the transfer of parcels of coded meaning from one text to another'.[9] What had begun as a footnote in my thesis developed into a detailed study of the afterlife of an object, in line with my ongoing interest in style and its reception across cultures and time.

I was also interested in broadening my understanding and scope of the superfluous and the decorative in art, concepts that recur within different areas of my research and discussions with artists, and that have also fed back into my academic activities. In March 2014 I co-convened a confer-ence with a colleague at Leeds entitled 'The Production of Ornament', exploring the production and reception of ornament over time and across cultures. Our call for papers attracted a broad range of scholars who shared an interest and concern for the place of ornament within, or more specifically outside, traditional formal and temporal categories. We addressed important questions raised by ornament and decoration and the middle ground they occupy in different art and architectural traditions and historiographies. One particular strength of the event was its trans-

---

[8]     Lara Eggleton, 'Reuse and Reception in the Life of a Sixteenth-century Chimneypiece', *Renaissance Studies* 30:3 (June 2016), 389–409.
[9]     Alexander Nagel and Christopher S. Wood, *Anachronic Renaissance* (New York: Zone Books, 2010), 178–9.

historical focus, which allowed scholars to discuss ideas in more abstract and thematic terms.[10]

Developing another strain of the thesis, Victorian travel encounters with the Alhambra led me to spend additional time looking at travel descriptions and testimonies, and the effects these have had on popular and critical historiographies of Islamic art and architecture of the premodern age.[11] Initially interested in the way that a sense of the Islamic Other emerged through these descriptions, I came to understand how this exotic but accessible frontier provided a new generation of sightseers with a glimpse of the Islamic world, without the inconvenience of long-distance travel or more threatening locales. This influx of tourism would have lasting implications for perceptions of Spain and its Muslim and Jewish heritage, which are closely tied to the historiography that has sprung up around it, from the eighteenth century to present day. These written and visual accounts also impacted upon the way that Muslim societies and their monuments have been and continue to be viewed by Euro-American audiences. Through the descriptions of early tourists, it is possible to gain a deeper understanding of pervasive models of speaking and writing about so called 'non-Western' architecture in the Western world. These accounts can also be cross-referenced with the formation of disciplines such as Art History, and popular and critical constructions of Otherness.

Through these further investigations, I have become increasingly interested in the phenomenon of experiencing objects – specifically how people approach, encounter and interpret historical monuments – and how these experiences shape our understanding of global cultures. This approach denies a fixed or constant view of the object by introducing human perception as an ever-shifting and affective force upon the material world, and it upon us. Taking a page from anthropologist Tim Ingold, the growth of embodied skills of perception and action can tell us much about changing relationships between humans, animals and other living and non-living things.[12] Rather than projecting backwards from an artwork or building as a way of understanding artist intent, adopting a 'being with

---

[10]    <https://follymatters.wordpress.com/2014/04/13/ornament-a-space-between/> (accessed 23 November 2018).

[11]    'History in the Making: The ornament of the Alhambra and the past-facing present', *Journal of Art Historiography* 6 (June 2012), ISSN 2042-4752; '"A living ruin": Palace, city and landscape in nineteenth-century travel descriptions of Granada', *Architecture Theory Review* 18:3 (December 2013), 372–87.

[12]    Tim Ingold, *Being Alive: Essays on movement, knowledge and description* (London and New York: Routledge, 2011).

things' approach affords insight into the processes, skills and materials that constitute meaning. Bill Brown's introduction of 'thing theory' and Jane Bennet's more recent forays into ecomaterialism are other examples of a growing branch of material studies that takes human/object relations into account.[13] Visual studies can play an important role in exposing the elaborate constructedness of human perception, challenging an anthropocentric view of the world. Fostering a deeper sensitivity to human/object encounters can help us see built and natural environments from different cultural perspectives, and thus circumvent dominant narratives within art and architectural histories. In my recent research this has helped me consider touristic accounts in terms of both passive and active forms of reflection, as travellers struggled to negotiate both familiar and exotic elements of foreign locales, within the limits of travel tourism. Whether through fascination, wonder and awe, or confusion, frustration and exhaustion, travellers' descriptions of the built environment reveal a highly reflexive process of situating – or failing to situate – Islamic monuments in relation to existing categories. In turn, their views influenced the expectations of other travellers, as well as popular perceptions of medieval non-Western art forms that are paradoxically situated in Western Europe.[14]

## Picking Up the Pieces

While the seeds of this object-led approach were planted in my PhD, it has taken much longer for them to take root, namely through the realisation of the importance of individual perspectives to a larger historiographic picture. Subsequent research has also consolidated for me the ever-interpretive, generative process of history-making, something that I also explore in my non-academic writing. My freelance activities in the arts, which include writing, workshops and consultancy, pre-date my research activities and have continued alongside it. Working in the art world gives me a wide creative berth where I can make wild and unsubstantiated observations and experiment with form and genre. Shortly after completing my PhD I started a blog, Folly Matters, which I use as a free platform for discussing art, artifice and fakery – a quest I playfully subtitled 'the monumental pursuit of pointlessness'.[15] I chose the folly,

[13] Bill Brown, 'Thing Theory', *Critical Inquiry* 28:1, 1–22; Jane Bennett, *Vibrant Matter: A political ecology of things* (Durham, NC: Duke University Press, 2010).
[14] Eggleton, '"A living ruin"'.
[15] <https://follymatters.wordpress.com/> (accessed 23 November 2018).

which can refer both to the architectural phenomenon of ornamental buildings and 'a foolish act', to serve as a vehicle for questioning the function of art and other forms of non-functional cultural production. A theme loose enough to allow commentary, reviews and collaborations in a responsive manner, it has served me well as a place to develop ideas without the restrictions of academic publishing. In the spirit of 'slogging' (the slow version of blogging), I average a post every two to three months, and have explored everything from field trips to folly gardens, to political farce and fake documents, to the creation of elaborate replicas in contemporary art. Sometimes the historical and contemporary overlap: I reviewed a contemporary work by Matthew Crawley in the form of a replica of the poster drums found dotted around Leeds, which the artist appropriately called *Temple*. A folly of a sort, I was interested in how the piece projected a subtle anti-commercialism while drawing on the ancient form of the monolith.[16]

My blog has also functioned as a platform for discussions with artists and other writers, where I can explore history, theory and practice beyond the limitations of traditional scholarship. In some cases this has led to further collaborations, such as the project 'Medieval helpdesk' that I co-curate with artist David Steans.[17] Since 2014, we've explored the intersection of the medieval and the contemporary through exhibitions and publications. We erected a gazebo at the 2015 International Medieval Congress in which we showcased the work of five contemporary artists whose work borrowed or dabbled in medieval themes or concepts (including a pedal-powered hurdy-gurdy in the shape of a gothic church, and a live anchorite). We were interested in engaging medieval scholars through the language of contemporary art, delving into the sacred and profane, the ritualistic and the superstitious, as dichotomies of enduring fascination. Since then, we have collaborated with the online art-writing platform Doggerland and the Bristol Biennial to produce a fabricated account of the medieval origins of the art biennale,[18] produced an artwork responding to the touristification of Richard III's Leicester for the group exhibition, 'Medieval-City One' at Two Queens Gallery,[19] and

---

[16]  <https://follymatters.wordpress.com/2013/07/20/temple-a-temporary-ruin/> (accessed 23 November 2018).

[17]  <http://www.medievalhelpdesk.co.uk/> (accessed 9 February 2018).

[18]  <http://www.doggerland.info/artistled/project/bristolbiennial/festivalisbiennis> (accessed 23 November 2018).

[19]  <https://2queens.com/exhibitions/medieval-city-one> (accessed 9 February 2018).

developed a piece for the 2018 exhibition 'As Much About Forgetting' at
Viborg Kunsthal, Denmark.

In 2014, my interest in follies dovetailed with a contemporary arts and
heritage project called 'The Follies of Youth', initiated by arts commis-
sioning body Pavilion and supported by The Heritage Lottery Fund and
Arts Council England.[20] A response to the tercentenary of the architect
and landscape designer Capability Brown, the project culminated in an
exhibition of historical research and contemporary art at The Calder,
a former textile mill within The Hepworth, Wakefield. My involve-
ment as a 'folly' began with a writing residency at the Good Hatchery,
an historic farmstead converted into an artist live/workspace in county
Offaly, Ireland, as part of a new commission by artist Ruth Lyons. With
a group of volunteers and the help of YouTube, we built a functioning
lime kiln as a way of doing hands-on research into early lime production. This formed the basis for Lyons's subsequent work, a large-scale
mirrored structure, which reflected limelight (a bright but highly flam-
mable source of light). The sculpture was shipped to Yorkshire and
placed by our group in a former Capability Brown-designed landscape,
Byram Park, located near disused limestone quarries and overlooked
by Ferrybridge coal power station. Lime production, along with peat
mining and other industrial processes, became a binding element in
both the geological and folkloric history of the Irish Midlands and the
English North, and formed the basis for my subsequent blog entry
inspired by the residency period.[21]

For the final exhibition at The Calder, Hepworth, which included
work by Lyons and three other artists, I was asked to design and imple-
mented a 'mapping exercise' – a kind of participatory reminisce event –
that involved engaging gallery visitors on the subjects of 'lost landscapes'.
Over the course of five days I invited visitors of all ages and abilities
to share their individual experience of local heritage landscapes, most
of them transformed by agricultural and industrial activity. I brought
together their responses in a 'fake history', a co-authored piece that demonstrated the creative act of selecting and assembling facts into a narrative that can then be understood as authoritative or 'official'. The piece
was posted to participants and launched at The Hepworth in 2015. My
background as an art and architectural historian was particularly relevant

[20]  < http://thefolliesofyouth.co.uk/> (accessed 23 November 2018).
[21]  <https://follymatters.wordpress.com/2014/09/02/breaking-earth/> (accessed
23 November 2018).

here, especially my approach to history as a malleable realm of interpretation. Drawing on my critical faculties and questioning the authority of official historical accounts, I worked with participants to forge new narratives and folklore, thereby fostering a sense of wonder and curiosity for a local history buried by industry and agriculture.

I worked with Pavilion again in 2015 on another Follies of Youth project, as part of the city-wide 'About Time' programme (running parallel to British Art Show 8 at Leeds Art Gallery), leading a group of eleven volunteers over a three-month period. During weekly discussions and a field trip to Temple Works (Marshall's Mill) in Holbeck, the group found inroads into the history of Leeds transport and textile production, accessing local archives and heritage sites, which led to the publication *Futures Past*, produced in collaboration with Leeds-based designer Anna Peaker. Volunteers used different art forms to express their ideas and research, including creative writing, drawing, screen printing, photography and video. Further emphasising the movement of time in both forward and backward directions, a participatory launch event at the Brunswick in January 2016 invited visitors to assemble a version of the book in an order of their choosing.

Such collaborations have contributed to the diversification and refining of certain strands of my research. In moving away from a single specialism that might have chained me to a particular monument, person or period, to the exclusion of others, I have chosen to pursue multiple themes and temporalities that at times cross-pollinate in delightfully creative ways. Art writing has been an effective way for me to explore ideas and write freely outside academia, which has in turn enriched and enlivened my research and teaching. Rather than thinking purely about objects and their histories, my collaborations with makers have allowed me to focus and linger on issues surrounding creative and material processes, and the drive to create art more generally. Moreover, it has made me think about how the past is received and interpreted by audiences, and how hierarchies of perception ultimately determine the value of things. Some further implications of this transhistorical thinking are outlined in my recent feature in *Art Monthly*, in which I discuss the prevalence of follies in contemporary art practice as a challenge (conscious or otherwise) to the extreme austerity and conservatism of our current political climate.[22]

These projects, collaborations and events reflect my investment in what the 'Slow Scholarship Manifesto' calls 'the deep patterns, structures and

[22]    Lara Eggleton, 'Folly', *Art Monthly*, issue 416 (May 2018).

ideas that are part of cultural foundations',[23] and, I would add, the inner, rumbling engines of artistic production and reception. Increasingly, I see my roles as an art writer and collaborator as equally important to my academic research, and integral to my continued interest in multiple subject areas. After all, if slow scholarship is to be likened to sharing a carefully prepared, organically grown meal in a leisurely fashion, it should be both nourishing and enjoyable, and communicate some of the passion and dedication that went into it. Much like ruin, its layers and complexity should inspire genuine dialogue and exchange, from which something original might emerge.

[23]   'Slow Scholarship: A manifesto', http://web.uvic.ca/~hist66/slowScholarship.

Slow Words

# *Translating* The Order of the World *in My Own Time*[1]

## JAMES PAZ

### On Slow Translation

Famously, the story of English poetry begins with eating words. Bede tells us that Cædmon devoured Christian teaching and Bible stories, and ruminated on them overnight, before converting those stories into the sweetest songs, like a cow chewing the cud and yielding milk.[2]

Over a thousand years later, as scholars started looking for slower, more ruminative ways of learning and writing they again turned to food and to metaphors of eating for inspiration. The manifesto for so-called 'slow scholarship' declares that:

> Slow scholarship is thoughtful, reflective, and the product of rumina-
> tion – a kind of field testing against other ideas. It is carefully prepared,
> with fresh ideas, local when possible, and is best enjoyed leisurely, on
> one's own or as part of a dialogue around a table with friends, family
> and colleagues. Like food, it often goes better with wine.[3]

This manifesto, which clearly draws on the Slow Food movement, was perhaps intended as a tongue-in-cheek corrective to the fast-paced, stress-driven culture of contemporary academia. Since then, the call for slower forms of scholarship has been taken up with (somewhat incongruous) vigour. The first book to articulate how the principles of the Slow movement might be adopted in the academy, *The Slow Professor*, by Maggie Berg and Barbara K. Seeber, demonstrates that slowing down need not be a retreat from everyday life, or a nostalgic return to the good old days.

---

[1]    This essay was first delivered as a paper in the second of two panels on 'Slow Scholarship in the Digital Age' at the Leeds International Medieval Congress, 2014. I am grateful to Catherine Karkov for organising these panels and inviting me to participate.

[2]    Book IV, Chapter 24 of Bede, *Ecclesiastical History of the English People*, ed. Bertram Colgrave and R.A.B. Mynors (Oxford: Clarendon Press, 1969), 418–19.

[3]    'Slow Scholarship: A manifesto' is available online: http://web.uvic.ca/~hist66/slowScholarship/

Rather, it can be a way of resisting the 'discourse of crisis' promoted by the corporate university, a sense of constant panic that leaves us feeling passive and helpless. Slowing down encourages a different kind of agency, a way of acting with purpose, taking the time for deliberation and reflection and dialogue, cultivating deep attention in our research.[4]

To date, then, the slow scholarship movement has considered how the act of slowing down can improve both working conditions and the quality of research produced in the university as a workplace. But I opened by creating a link between slow scholarship and the poets and poetry of the distant past. I am interested in how slow scholarship might improve my knowledge of early medieval literature; but am equally interested in how the practices of that far-off age might inform my own ways of working. As Karen Jolly argues elsewhere in this collection, slow scholarship finds a counterpart in the painstaking handcrafting of medieval manuscripts (pp. 125–41). Clare Lees and Gillian Overing have highlighted the cognitive processes involved not only in making manuscripts but in remaking their meaning through the pre-eminently slow practices of rumination, contemplation and meditation in medieval monasticism.[5] Thus, the Old English texts that we now tend to encounter in modern textbooks or anthologies were not only produced but consumed slowly – and when I say *consumed* I am deliberately returning to the metaphor of eating. Worms ate the words of medieval manuscripts, but so too did human readers meditating upon sacred texts. The process of *ruminatio* drew parallels between a scholar digesting written material and a cow chewing cud or a bee making honey.[6]

Although *ruminatio* is not something we consciously cultivate in the twenty-first century, it still resonates with the work that scholars and teachers of Old English literature must do. We cannot teach undergraduate students to 'close read' an Old English poem in the same way that they might read a modern novel: each word must be defined and redefined; each sound pronounced properly; each line ordered and reordered. The difficulty of Old English stops us in our tracks, so that reading is sometimes indistinguishable from translating. Even the trained medievalist

[4]     Maggie Berg and Barbara K. Seeber, *The Slow Professor* (Toronto: University of Toronto Press, 2016), 11.
[5]     Clare Lees and Gillian Overing, 'The Collaborative Spiral: The art of early medieval slow scholarship', unpublished paper delivered at the International Medieval Congress, University of Leeds, 2014.
[6]     Michael Camille, *Image on the Edge: The margins of medieval art* (Cambridge, MA: Harvard University Press, 1992), 63–64.

encounters many knotty passages, over which she must pause and ponder. The same is true for accomplished poets. Seamus Heaney described the act of translating *Beowulf* as 'labour-intensive work, scriptorium-slow'.[7] Fiona Sampson, commenting on the translations she produced for *The Word Exchange*, acknowledges how the arduousness of the task can create a sense of intimacy with an otherwise distant poetry: 'I recognized how dictionary "finger-work" – with all the humility about the original language it implied – had got me tracing the original poem's actual thought and music.'[8] Old English confronts us with words and phrases that we can only half hear now, but there is pleasure and a sense of fulfilment in chiselling away at them until a strange likeness emerges.

A confession: in my own time, I have been working slowly, and painstakingly, on a collection of translations from Old English into what will eventually be modern English verse (or an attempt at verse). I have rendered most of these poems into coherent prose, but my translations are still mere drafts, mostly incomplete and imperfect. The collection is unlikely to be finished within the next decade, or two. I translate not with the REF (Research Excellence Framework) in mind, but almost as an extracurricular pastime. And I suspect that most Anglo-Saxonists, or at least those who work in English departments, have something similar hidden away in a drawer or saved on a computer. In their chapter on 'research and understanding' Berg and Seeber advise academics to accept that quality matters more than quantity, and to *wait* before publishing the work they have written.[9] Of course, delaying publication can have serious consequences when it comes to REF submissions. Yet (as far as I am aware) translation does not 'count' and is not 'counted' in the same way as monographs or articles. What is more, the act of translation is situated between critical and creative practice, the professional and the amateur; it complicates departmental divisions between language and literature; and it is at once early medieval scholarship and contemporary writing.

I chip away at my translations alone, often at daybreak – though they are also cross-temporal collaborations with Anglo-Saxon poets, or *scopas*, shapers like Cædmon chewing over pre-existing material, translators as much as creators. Whatever one believes about his or her creative

---

[7]    Seamus Heaney, 'Introduction', in *Beowulf: A verse translation*, trans. Seamus Heaney, ed. Daniel Donoghue (London: Norton, 2002), xxxiii.

[8]    Fiona Sampson, 'On Translating Old English Poetry', in *The Word Exchange: Anglo-Saxon poems in translation*, ed. Greg Delanty and Michael Matto (London: Norton, 2011), 536.

[9]    Berg and Seeber, *Slow Professor*, 64–5.

talents and poetic licence, the translator is always duty-bound to convey the sense, and arguably the sound, of the source text. Some translators, such as Craig Williamson, take a humble view of the process, seeing the primary purpose of translation as inspiring new readers 'to think about learning Old English in an effort to return to the originals where the real source of power and grandeur resides'.[10] On the other hand, the historical and cultural moment inhabited by the translator always affects how he or she interprets the older source text. As Hugh Magennis has argued in relation to translating *Beowulf*, each version is necessarily situated within its own time and context, for the very text of *Beowulf* (and indeed other Old English poetry) is not a fixed, stable entity but has been 'modified in the light of advances in scholarship'. This pertains to the micro-level of translating individual words and phrases, and in deciding how to render the form of the original, as well as to the macro-level of relating to the poem's overall style and status, the themes and ideas it contains, the worldviews it expresses.[11] Translations of *Beowulf* therefore 'age'. William Morris's *Beowulf* is clearly not the same text as Seamus Heaney's *Beowulf*.

One poem in particular – *The Order of the World* – has led me to contemplate what it means to convey an ancient poem slowly, across a long stretch of my own lifetime but also across a long stretch of historical time. What can be gained and what gets lost through the act of 'slow' translation? What happens when *my own time* – however you want to understand that ambiguous phrase – is expanded?

## Translating *The Order of the World*

*The Order of the World*, also known as *The Wonders of Creation* or, more recently, *A Song of the Cosmos*, might not be recognised as one of the canonical poems of Old English literature.[12] Yet it is probably one of the most difficult. I will start by admitting that I do not understand this poem. And I am not alone. For many scholars and poets, it is one of the

---

[10]   Craig Williamson, *Beowulf and Other Old English Poems* (Philadelphia, PA: University of Pennsylvania Press, 2011), 18.

[11]   Hugh Magennis, *Translating Beowulf: Modern versions in English verse* (Cambridge: D.S. Brewer, 2011), 2–4. Magennis is drawing on poststructuralist translation theory to make this point. See, for example, Umberto Eco, *Mouse or Rat? Translation as negotiation* (London: Weidenfeld & Nicolson, 2003).

[12]   It is titled *A Song of the Cosmos* in Daniel Tobin's recent translation of it for *The Word Exchange*, ed. Delanty and Matto, 238–45. I have also consulted the translation by R.M. Liuzza in *Old English Poetry: An Anthology*, ed. and trans. R.M. Liuzza (London: Broadview Press, 2014), 63–6.

trickiest Old English texts to interpret, let alone translate. Therefore, I am not going to offer a fully formed reading but will instead describe a process – a process of getting to know this text through slow translation.

Before scrutinising *The Order of the World* word by word, I wanted to get some sense of its shape, to have an image in my mind of how it is patterned, how it has been crafted into a thing that we can identify as a 'poem'. For Robert DiNapoli, it comprises, at first glance, 'a vivid but rambling hymn on the glories of the created cosmos, studded with homiletic commonplaces and ringing with faint echoes of Germanic wisdom poetry'.[13] So, the poem takes as its theme the entire cosmos; it contains the whole of creation, and conveys that universe to us in an incoherent style, drawing on at least two different traditions and worldviews. This is clearly not a text for the fainthearted. The poem itself appears aware of the challenge it sets:

> Leorna þas lare.     Ic þe lungre sceal
> meotudes mægensped        maran gesecgan,
> þonne þu hygecræftig        in hreþre mæge
> mode gegripan.    Is sin meaht forswiþ. (23–26)

(Learn this lore! Swiftly I must speak to you of the measurer's abundant might, too much for you, spirit-skilled in heart, to grasp within your mind. His power is too great.)

But perhaps it also provides us with a method for understanding the cosmos it contains and conveys:

> Forþon scyle ascian,     se þe on elne leofað,
> deophydig mon,        dygelra gesceafta,
> bewritan in gewitte        wordhordes cræft,
> fæstnian ferðsefan,        þencan forð teala;
> ne sceal þæs aþreotan        þegn modigne,
> þæt he wislice     woruld fulgonge. (17–22)

(Therefore the deep-minded one who lives with courage must inquire into the secret shape of things, inscribe in the mind the craft of the word-hoard, fasten the thinking-force, consider correctly; the mindful thane must not grow weary of this, to wisely perfect the world.)

---

[13]   Robert DiNapoli, 'The Heart of the Visionary Experience: *The Order of the World* and its place in the Old English canon', *English Studies* 79:2 (1998), 97–108, at 97.

Could I adopt and adapt this approach as a way into understanding *The Order of the World*? I drew up a set of working methods for myself, a manner of inquiry and mental inscription that would lead, step by step, to a slowly crafted translation. Each dawn, I would return, unwearied, to the act of re-creation, following these instructions:

- Read the Old English text. Read every single word. If any word strikes you as unusual, or attractive, or tricky, consult a dictionary of Old English. Compare and criticise the dictionaries. Recognise that a dictionary is merely a device for producing infinite linguistic chains. Words mean other words, old and new. Pursue these paths but do not get lost in the labyrinth. It leads to unreality. Should you lose your way amid the dictionaries, say the word *leoht* and look at the sun; or *þeostre* and close your eyes. Ask: has the cosmos itself changed or only the words we use to know it?
- When you have read the words, recognise that you are reading an edition. Read *through* the edition. Look at the spacing employed, pay special attention to any italicised words, question capitalisation, never accept punctuation. Look at the manuscript, whenever possible. Look at the inky script, and at other markings that are also a kind of poetry: burns, scratches, tears, stitches, finger-stains. Consider the other texts in the manuscript. *The Order of the World* is found in the Exeter Book. What does it share space with?
- Now draft an ambiguous translation, keeping your options open.[14] You will need to make a choice at a later stage, capturing words upon paper. But you must not lose richness or variety of meaning too soon:

| Wilt þu, fus hæle, | fremdne monnan, |
| wisne woðboran | wordum gretan, |
| fricgan felageongne | ymb forðgesceaft (1–3) |

Do you wish (will you?), hurrying (eager, ready, ready for death, dying) hero (brave man, healer?), to greet with words, the foreign (strange) man (pun on moon?), the wise speaker (poet, voice-bearer; *woð?* mad-possessed- inspired-), to ask (discover, learn by asking) the wide- (far-) travelled one about creation (continuing creation, the future world, things to come).

---

[14]  The idea of an 'ambiguous' translation is partly inspired by Craig Williamson's working method, as described in his introduction to *Beowulf and Other Old English Poems*, 1–18.

- Start to pin words down. But contemplate the words chosen, exchange them if necessary, keep wrestling with and varying words (*wordum wrixlan*, as the Anglo-Saxons said):

Do you wish, *hurrying* hero, to greet with words, the *strange* man, the wise *poet*, to ask the *wide-travelled* one about *creation*?

Do you wish, *dying* hero, to greet with words, the *foreign* man, the wise *speech-bearer*, to ask the *far-travelled* one about *things to come*?

- Observe the translated line, and then sound it out, chew it over, taste each word as it trickles across your tongue. If the verse stalls or stutters, if the flow feels forced, or if it is forgettable, something needs to be changed.
- Memorise each line, and then:
- Link it to another; if there are blanks in your memory, if a link is broken, something is wrong. Go back, start over.
- Finally, question your own assumptions, the cosmology you inhabit as a translator. What have you brought to the text and how has this transformed, or distorted, it? In return, what has the text done to you, as a translator? Has your cosmology been destabilised in any way?

By following this method, what I found was that the difficulty of the text was not only an effect of historical distance. It soon became apparent that some kind of 'test' of poetic skill was built into the poem. As with many Old English poems, *The Order* demonstrates a fondness for wordplay and punning, which makes it tricky to capture lexical meanings. I had encountered this before with other Exeter Book poems, such as the riddles. But, at a formal level, it was the syntax of this poem that presented a different kind of challenge. In his edition and translation of the poem, E.G. Stanley notes that the text relies not on pithily expressed gnomes but on the 'sentence paragraph'. Translators struggle to handle these sentences, bound as we are by the neater grammatical punctuation of modern languages. Conversely, the manuscript text of *The Order* uses the *punctus* very sparingly.[15]

Obviously, my preconceived ideas about 'poetic lines' were misguided. In my attempt to translate *The Order* line by line, I found myself grappling with sentences that did not want to conclude, sentences that started

---

[15]   E.G. Stanley, '*The Wonder of Creation*: A new edition and translation, with discussion of problems', *Anglia* 131:4 (2013), 475–508, at 477.

as if they were questions (*Wilt þu…*) but which spiralled on and on for
such a length of time and space that they seemed to transform themselves
into exclamations. I sensed a certain tension between the mouth that
speaks, the hand that writes and the mind that imagines and organises.
Indeed, when striving to memorise each line and mentally link one line
with another, it occurred to me that a deliberate mnemonic challenge
– testing the limits and possibilities of memory – may well be another
feature of this poem. The opening 'paragraph' appears to introduce two
personae, one of whom (the *wis woðbora*) is wiser, more experienced,
widely travelled, while the other (the *fus hæle*) is the novice in receipt
of that wisdom and experience. The latter 'persona' is addressed in the
second person, inviting the reader or audience to identify with their position. In one long breathless sentence, we are simultaneously being asked
and ordered to speak about and to mentally inscribe the mystery of creation. A little further down, at line 19, we are instructed to 'bewritan in
gewitte wordhordes cræft' (inscribe in the mind the craft of the word-
hoard). This line alludes to a consciously cultivated mnemonic device, the
creation of mental images 'inscribed in a physical way upon that part of
the body which constitutes memory'.[16]

I also found that the process (translating) and product (translation)
started to fold into each other. What was revealed through my slow translation of *The Order of the World* was at once a new, old poem and a way of
creating a new, old poem. For the role and the method of the Old English
*scop* is provided in the text itself, albeit in subtle and enigmatic ways. We
are presented with a *hycgende mon* able to hold the entire world within
their breast, or seat of thought, and who is linked to shadowy figures from
the ancient past:

> Is þara anra gehwam       orgeate tacen,
> þam þurh wisdom       woruld ealle con
> behabban on hreþre,       hycgende mon,
> þæt geara iu,       gliwes cræfte,
> mid gieddingum       guman oft wrecan,
> rincas rædfæste;       cuþon ryht sprecan,
> þæt a fricgende       fira cynnes
> ond secgende       searoruna gespon
> a gemyndge mæst       monna wiston. (8–16)

---

16   Mary Carruthers, *The Book of Memory: A study of memory in medieval culture*
(Cambridge: Cambridge University Press, 1990), 16.

(Each of these is a manifest token
to the *contemplator* —
the one who, through wisdom,
knows how to hold the whole world in his breast,
what long ago, with glee-craft and songs,
men often recited, those well-counselled warriors;
they knew right-speech, so that,
by always *inquiring* and *uttering*
the allure of artful *mysteries*,
they were ever mindful:
of the kindred of men, knowing the most.)

Critics have argued over whether these ancient figures are a skilled elite of Germanic oral poets, or Biblical psalmists and prophets.[17] Like many of the *scopas* found in Old English literature, they seem to exist in a semi-mythical bygone age (*geara iu*) imbued with an air of awe and authority, which represented the Anglo-Saxons' own mental modelling of their ancestral past.[18] But, again, in a rather self-reflexive way we might compare this vagueness to the modern translator's connection with the Anglo-Saxon poets of days gone by: were they singers, harpists, scribes, thanes, monks, pagan or Christian, oral or literate, men or women, all or none of the above?[19]

The poet proceeds to explain how these ancient figures worked: the text describes a process of learning by asking (*fricgende*), speaking (*secgende*) and remembering (*gemynde*). *The Order of the World* is not only a poem about poetry, but specifically about translation. Following the opening lines, which concern themselves with the process of making poetry, we encounter an internal poem largely based on Psalm 18, and described as a *herespel*. According to Ruth Wehlau, the sort of poetic expansion found in the *herespel* demonstrates a response to both the language of the original text and to its images, and 'this aspect of rumination would involve not only the "digestion" of the text's doctrinal significance, but also imaginative play with the imagery, a re-working of the literal language of

---

[17]   For a summary, see DiNapoli, 'The Heart of the Visionary Experience', 99.

[18]   John D. Niles, 'The Myth of the Anglo-Saxon Oral Poet', *Western Folklore* 62 (2003), 7–61.

[19]   For the ways in which modern conceptions of Anglo-Saxon poets have been shaped by Romantic ideas about the oral bard, see Roberta Frank, 'The Search for the Anglo-Saxon Oral Poet', *Bulletin of the John Rylands Library* 75 (1993), 11–36. For a more recent study of historical Anglo-Saxon poets and their social roles, see Emily V. Thornbury, *Becoming a Poet in Anglo-Saxon England* (Cambridge: Cambridge University Press, 2014).

the Bible'.[20] Therefore, *The Order of the World* seems to give us a slow, reflective way of translating – a process of learning through deep inquiry, knowing through memorisation and contemplation, and crafting through rumination – which would seem ideally suited to the aims and ethics of slow scholarship.

But this slow process, detailed and rigorous though it is, may not function *in my own time* – may not lead to the kind of understanding – the kind of knowing – the kind of truth – that the Old English poem wants us to draw from it. When we have only fragmented knowledge of a far-off age, something must go missing across the seas of time. How can a modern scholar remember the long-lost wisdom and accurately re-create the working method of an Old English *scop*? What is it I am picturing or imagining in my mind, and what sort of reality are these images drawn from? The *scop* represented in *The Order* is more than a mundane craftsman. He or she has access to special lore, beyond the ken of ordinary human beings.

The poem opens by challenging the listener – who is placed in the position of an aspiring poet – to greet with words the *wisne woðboran*. As Jeff Opland points out, the etymology of the first half of the compound *woðboran* shares a common Indo-European root with the Old English word *wod* ('mad' or 'possessed'), the name of the god Woden, and the Latin word *vates*, which can mean both 'poet' and 'seer'.[21] What is more, the aspiring poet must question this *woðbora* about *forðgesceaft* – a term used in wisdom poetry to indicate a profound foreknowledge normally exclusive to God.

The *Order of the World* presents the *scop* as a visionary sage, able to receive divine inspiration and glimpse the unfolding pattern of creation, unbound by linear time. We can add to this picture the claim that those ancient figures to whom poets of the present are linked were able to speak *searoruna gespon* – cunning secrets, tricky runes, skilful counsels, artful mysteries? Armed with these special powers, the *scopas* of old *cupon ryht sprecan* – knew right speech or how to speak in the right way. For DiNapoli, the author of *The Order of the World* 'seems to see poetic language as neither an inert nor merely ornamental vessel for truth, but as its

---

[20]   Ruth Wehlau, 'Rumination and Re-Creation: Poetic instruction in *The Order of the World*', *Florilegium* 13 (1994), 65–77, at 72.
[21]   Jeff Opland, *Anglo-Saxon Oral Poetry: A study of the traditions* (New Haven and London: Yale University Press, 1980), 250. Cf. Thornbury, *Becoming a Poet*, 25.

very embodiment'.[22] *The Order of the World* is not merely a creation that speaks of creation. It somehow embodies Creation itself. It is not simply a song *of the* cosmos; it is song *and* cosmos.

And yet, when translating *The Order of the World* in, or for, my own time, I must remain aware that I am evoking a cosmos that is now, in the words of C.S. Lewis, a discarded image: a geocentric cosmology over-turned by the Copernican revolution, a Creation that many would no longer consider to have been created.[23] How can the poetic language of the Anglo-Saxon *scop* still embody knowledge, even truth, when the crea-tion of which they sing has lost its firm foundations?

> Gehyr nu þis herespel      ond þinne hyge gefæstna.
> Hwæt, on frymþe gescop      fæder ælmihtig,
> heah hordes weard,      heofon ond eorðan,
> sæs sidne grund,      sweotule gesceafte,
> þa nu in þam þream      þurh þeodnes hond
> heaþ ond hebbaþ      þone halgan blæd. (37–42)

(Hear, now, this praise-song and fasten your heart.
*Hwæt.* The father almighty, holder of high hosts,
shaped at the start the heaven and earth,
the sea's broad bed, and everything you see,
which now, hardened through the lord's hand,
heightens and heaves up the holy fruits.)

From this perspective, God has created the universe as a manifest sign. Through contemplative reading of this wondrous Creation, the poet is able to digest the book of the world and reproduce it through the medium of poetry. Even the alliteratively linked lines convey a sense of Boethian stability of creation:

> Forþon swa teofenede,      se þe teala cuþe,
> dæg wiþ nihte,      deop wið hean,
> lyft wið lagustream,      lond wiþ wæge,
> flod wið flode,      fisc wið yþum.
> Ne waciað þas geweorc,      ac he hi wel healdeð (82–86)

[22]   DiNapoli, 'The Heart of the Visionary Experience', 102.
[23]   The 'discarded image' was a term famously coined by C.S. Lewis to describe the synthesis of medieval theology, science and history into a single, complex, harmonious mental model of the universe. See further C.S. Lewis, *The Discarded Image: An introduction to Medieval and Renaissance literature* (Cambridge: Cambridge University Press, 1964).

The very metre is self-reflexively embodying knowledge about, and
the truth of, a firmly fixed creation. Of course, the Boethian view of a
stable creation had to be reconciled in Anglo-Saxon Christian thought
with the visible evidence of a decaying world, a sign that the fixedness
of Creation would last only until Doomsday. As another Exeter Book
poem clearly declares, 'Swa þes middangeard ealra dogra gehwam dreoseð
and fealleþ' (So this middle-earth declines and falls each and every day)
(*The Wanderer*, lines 62–63). And I wonder about that innocuous little
word *wið*, used so often in Old English to mark separation or to indicate
opposition or friction. Only a kind of anti-translation can convey this
underlying corrosion:

And so, the one who knows well, fixed
day *against* night, the deeps *against* the heights,
sky *against* sea-stream, land *against* water,
flood *against* flood, fish *against* waves.

*Ne waciað þas geweorc,*         *ac he hi wel healdeð*

All works must weaken, however hard we hold them.

The Old English poet may have had Doomsday in mind. Yet this stable
Creation did weaken in a less apocalyptic sense, eroded by Copernicus
decentralising the Earth, by Galileo spying the moons of Jupiter through
his telescope, by Newton pondering beneath an apple tree – the geocentric, or theocentric, cosmos slowly decaying until it was discarded entirely
and became only a beautiful but false image, artifice and no longer truth.
In *The Order of the World*, the shining sun represents the height of glorious knowledge:

Lifgendra gehwam          leoht forð biereð
bronda beorhtost,           ond his brucan mot
æghwylc on eorþan,        þe him eagna gesihð
sigora soðcyning            syllan wolde. (64–67)

(For each of the living it bears forth its light,
the brightest of brands and a gift to everyone
on earth, those who the true king of victory
would give eyes to see.)

But its descent is also described, the darkening of knowledge:

Forþon nænig fira          þæs frod leofað
þæt his mæge æspringe          þurh his ægne sped witan,
hu geond grund færeð          goldtorht sunne
in þæt wonne genip          under wætra geþring,
oþþe hwa þæs leohtes          londbuende
brucan mote,          siþþan heo ofer brim hweorfeð. (76–81)

(And so no one living among us has the wisdom
to know of his waning through his own means,
how the gold-bright sun fares beyond the earth,
into dark shadow, beneath the welling waves,
or who of the land-dwellers can receive that light,
after it departs over the ocean's edge.)

Perhaps my concerns about 'not understanding' *The Order of the World*
are unfounded, since the poem has a sense of unknowing built into it.
The movement of the sun into another place (the antipodes) and time
(as day passes into night) to be received by a mysterious group of earth-
dwellers, anticipates a dark and secret future, a loss of meaning across
long ages.

If Creation itself can decline, so too can the created poem. Poetic
language can link together disparate elements but it cannot hold them
together forever. We are not only dealing with the fallibility of human
memory here. *The Order* is a written text, recorded in a manuscript on
leaves of parchment. The Exeter Book is torn here and there, scored with
knife strokes, stained by fish glue, riddled in places with wormholes, and
if we burrow through the pages of that same Exeter Book, we find a
certain enigma:

Moððe word fræt.          Me þæt þuhte
wrætlicu wyrd,          þa ic þæt wundor gefrægn,
þæt se wyrm forswealg          wera gied sumes,
þeof in þystro,          þrymfæstne cwide
ond þæs strangan staþol.          Stælgiest ne wæs
wihte þy gleawra,          þe he þam wordum swealg.

(A moth ate words—
I thought it strange to hear,
and a wonder of fate,
that a worm in darkness
can thieve a man's fine riddle,
swallow his song,
sip eloquence and feast on its foundation.

And yet that stealthy guest
who dines on stolen words will leave no wiser.)[24]

The book moth riddle may be read as a metaphor for a monk or student
unsuccessfully ruminating on the written word,[25] but it is also a meditation on transience and entropy, whereby even carefully preserved creations
can be eaten away by time and fate, *wyrm* and *wyrd*.

Anglo-Saxon views of the cosmos are often dismissed as pre-scientific.
But even in our supposedly post-Renaissance, post-Enlightenment world
there remain many things beyond the grasp of mortal minds. Our own
cosmological models might not be as fixed, as stable, as we imagine. The
future may yet discard our images of the universe. In the epilogue to *The
Discarded Image*, Lewis recognised that we ought to be wary of regarding
the early modern cosmological 'revolutions' as a simple progress from
error to truth. Models of the cosmos reflect the prevalent psychology
of an age almost as much as they reflect the state of that age's scientific
knowledge.[26] Cosmology simply means 'words about the universe'. Ruth
Padel has reflected upon the relationship between the language of poetry
and the language of science, reminding us that poetry was the first written
way in which humans questioned what the world is made of and how it
came to be. Poetry and science have more in common than revealing the
secrets of nature, though. Both depend on metaphor, which is as crucial
to scientific discovery as it is to lyric poetry since 'a new metaphor is a
new mapping of the world'. Yet the deepest thing science and poetry
share, perhaps, is 'the way they can tolerate uncertainty'. They both strive
towards truth without ever reaching that destination.[27]

As the days and months and years pass by, *The Order of the World*
takes shape. Each dawn, I return, unwearied, to my slow translation, to
the act of re-creation. I think of an anonymous Anglo-Saxon *scop* lying
beneath a barrow, clutching a lyre as they prepare, perpetually, to travel
into an undiscovered country. Light always departs over the ocean's edge,
and time itself ensures that poets and prophets, philosophers and cos-

---

[24]    Translation by Jane Hirshfield in *The Word Exchange*, ed. Delanty and Matto,
323.

[25]    Mercedes Salvador-Bello, *Isidorean Perceptions of Order: The Exeter Book
riddles and medieval Latin enigmata* (Morgantown: West Virginia University Press,
2015), 356–7.

[26]    Lewis, *Discarded Image*, 222.

[27]    Ruth Padel writing in *The Guardian* on 'The science of poetry, the poetry
of science', Friday, 9 December 2011; https://www.theguardian.com/books/2011/
dec/09/ruth-padel-science-poetry (accessed 8 June 2019).

mologists, singers and thinkers and dreamers alike, must pass out of sight, beyond all maps and mappings of the world, to embrace the ultimate realm of unknowing.

## The Wonder of Creation
## (or, work in progress)

### The Order of the World

Wilt þu, fus hæle,           fremdne monnan,
  wisne woðboran               wordum gretan,
  fricgan felageongne            ymb forðgesceaft,
  biddan þe gesecge           sidra gesceafta
  cræftas cyndelice           cwichrerende,
  þa þe dogra gehwam            þurh dom godes
  bringe wundra fela          wera cneorissum!


Is þara anra gehwam            orgeate tacen,
  þam þurh wisdom             woruld ealle con
  behabban on hreþre,           hycgende mon,
  þæt geara iu,             gliwes cræfte,
  mid gieddingum              guman oft wrecan,
  rincas rædfæste;            cuþon ryht sprecan,
  þæt a fricgende            fira cynnes
  ond secgende             searoruna gespon
  a gemyndge mæst            monna wiston.



Forþon scyle ascian,           se þe on elne leofað,
  deophydig mon,             dygelra gesceafta,
  bewritan in gewitte            wordhordes cræft,
  fæstnian ferðsefan,            þencan forð teala;
  ne sceal þæs aþreotan           þegn modigne,
  þæt he wislice          woruld fulgonge.



Leorna þas lare.      Ic þe lungre sceal
  meotudes mægensped           maran gesecgan,
  þonne þu hygecræftig           in hreþre mæge
  mode gegripan.      Is sin meaht forswiþ.


Nis þæt monnes gemet           moldhrerendra,
  þæt he mæge in hreþre        his heah geweorc
  furþor aspyrgan           þonne him frea sylle
  to ongietanne          godes agen bibod;

## The Wonder of Creation

Will you, hastening hero, hail a stranger
with words, welcome the wise speech-bearer,
question the far-questing one about events to come,
ask that he speak of the spacious creations,
of their life-quickening capacities,
which every day under the ordinance of God
bring many wonders to generations of men?

Each of these is a manifest token
to the contemplator —
the one who, through wisdom,
knows how to hold the whole world in his breast,
what long ago, with glee-craft and songs,
men often recited, those well-counselled warriors;
they knew right-speech, so that,
by always inquiring and uttering
the allure of artful mysteries,
they were ever mindful:
of the kindred of men, knowing the most.

And so the deep-minded one who lives with courage
must ask about the secret shape of things,
inscribe in mind the word-hoard's craft,
fasten the thinking-force, consider correctly;
the mindful thane must not grow weary of this,
to wisely fulfil his worldly ways.

Listen.

Learn this lore! Swiftly I must speak to you
of the measurer's abundant might,
too much for you, spirit-skilled in heart,
to grasp within your mind. His power is too great.

It is not the measure of earth-moving man
to search the high work any
further than the father allows him
to know through the lord's own law;

ac we sculon þoncian        þeodne mærum
awa to ealdre,        þæs þe us se eca cyning
on gæste wlite        forgiefan wille
þæt we eaðe magon        upcund rice
forð gestigan,        gif us on ferðe geneah
ond we willað healdan        heofoncyninges bibod.

Gehyr nu þis herespel        ond þinne hyge gefæstna.

Hwæt, on frymþe gescop        fæder ælmihtig,
heah hordes weard,        heofon ond eorðan,
sæs sidne grund,        sweotule gesceafte,
þa nu in þam þream        þurh þeodnes hond
heaþ ond hebbaþ        þone halgan blæd.

Forþon eal swa teofanade,        se þe teala cuþe,
æghwylc wiþ oþrum;        sceoldon eal beran
stiþe stefnbyrd,        swa him se steora bibead
missenlice gemetu        þurh þa miclan gecynd.

Swa hi to worulde        wlite forþ berað
dryhtnes duguþe        ond his dæda þrym,
lixende lof        in þa longan tid,
fremmaþ fæstlice        frean ece word
in þam frumstole        þe him frea sette,
hluttor heofones weard,        healdað georne
mere gemære;        meaht forð tihð
heofoncondelle        ond holmas mid,
laþað ond lædeþ        lifes agend
in his anes fæþm        ealle gesceafta.

Swa him wideferh        wuldor stondeþ,
ealra demena        þam gedefestan,
þe us þis lif gescop,        ond þis leohte beorht
cymeð morgna gehwam        ofer misthleoþu
wadan ofer wægas        wundrum gegierwed,
ond mid ærdæge        eastan snoweð
wlitig ond wynsum        wera cneorissum;
lifgendra gehwam        leoht forð biereð
bronda beorhtost,        ond his brucan mot
æghwylc on eorþan,        þe him eagna gesihð
sigora soðcyning        syllan wolde.
Gewiteð þonne mid þy wuldre        on westrodor
forðmære tungol        faran on heape,

but we must thank the renowned ruler
always across time, so that the eternal king
may decide to grant us grace of soul
and then we may easily ascend to the celestial realm,
should we be worthy of spirit and willingly
keep the heaven-king's law.

Hear, now, this praise-song and secure your heart.

The father almighty, holder of high hosts,
shaped at the start the heaven and earth,
the sea's broad bed, and everything you see,
which now, hardened through the lord's hand,
heightens and heaves up his holy abundance.

The one who readily knows therefore bound
each thing with another; they all must follow
a strict course, as their steersman instructed them,
in various measures, through many generations.

So they bear forth beauty into the world,
the master's magnificence and the might of his deeds,
shining praise into the long age,
perpetually performing the lord's eternal word
in that first throne, which the father fixed for them,
glorious guardian of heaven; they eagerly hold
their great circuit; his power propels
the candles of heaven and with them the waves,
the lord of life calls and leads
all creatures into his own embrace.

So glory stands with him for all time,
with the most just of judges,
who shaped this life for us, and this bright light
which comes every morning over misty cliffs
to drift over the waves, wondrously adorned,
and at daybreak hastens from the east,
beautiful and blissful for generations of men;
for each of the living it bears forth its light,
the brightest of brands and a gift to everyone
on earth, those who the true king
of victory would give eyes to see.
It glides then in its glory, into the western sky,
the most splendid star, to fare unfathomably,

oþþæt on æfenne          ut garsecges
grundas paþeð,           glom oþer cigð;
niht æfter cymeð,           healdeð nydbibod
halgan dryhtnes.           Heofontorht swegl
scir gescyndeð          in gesceaft godes
under foldan fæþm,           farende tungol.


Forþon nænig fira          þæs frod leofað
þæt his mæge æspringe           þurh his ægne sped witan,
hu geond grund færeð           goldtorht sunne
in þæt wonne genip           under wætra geþring,
oþþe hwa þes leohtes           londbuende
brucan mote,          siþþan heo ofer brim hweorfeð.


Forþon swa teofenede,          se þe teala cuþe,
dæg wiþ nihte,          deop wið hean,
lyft wið lagustream,           lond wiþ wæge,
flod wið flode,          fisc wið yþum.



Ne waciað þas geweorc,          ac he hi wel healdeð;
stondað stiðlice          bestryþed fæste
miclum meahtlocum           in þam mægenþrymme
mid þam sy ahefed           heofon ond eorþe.


Beoð þonne eadge          þa þær in wuniað,
hyhtlic is þæt heorðwerud.           þæt is herga mæst,
eadigra unrim,          engla þreatas.
Hy geseoð symle          hyra sylfra cyning,
eagum on wlitað,          habbað æghwæs genoh.
Nis him wihte won,           þam þe wuldres cyning
geseoþ in swegle;          him is symbel ond dream
ece unhwylen          eadgum to frofre.


Forþon scyle mon gehycgan          þæt he meotude hyre;
æghwylc ælda bearna          forlæte idle lustas,
læne lifes wynne,          fundige him to lissa blisse,
forlæte heteniþa          gehwone sigan
mid synna fyrnum,          fere him to þam sellan rice.

until in the evening it roams the regions
of the outer seas, calling forth another gloom;
night comes soon after, keeping to the command
of the holy lord. The heaven-bright brilliance,
the travelling star, speeds into the
Shaper's creation, under the earth's surface.

And so, no one living among us holds the wisdom
to know of their waning through their own means,
how the gold-bright sun fares beyond the earth,
into dark shadow, beneath the welling waves,
or who of the land-dwellers can receive that light,
after it departs over the ocean's edge.

And so, the one who knows well fixed
day with night, the deeps against the heights,
sky with sea-stream, land against water,
flood with flood, fish against waves.

All works must weaken, however hard we hold them.

Yet His works will not weaken, for He grasps them tight;
they stand steadfast, securely fastened,
by a great binding of might in the glory
by which heaven and earth are held up.

Those who abide there are blessed,
that household is hearth-happy.
That is the greatest of hosts,
countless saints and crowds of angels.
Their eyes alight on their everlasting king.
They have their fill of everything –
feasting and merriment forevermore –
They want for nothing,
those who witness the wonder of heaven.

And so,
take hold of your mind and obey the measurer:
let go of idle desires, the fleeting lusts of life;
let your longings lead you to loving bliss,
let hateful hostility,
each spiteful sin,
sink away,
for a better world awaits.

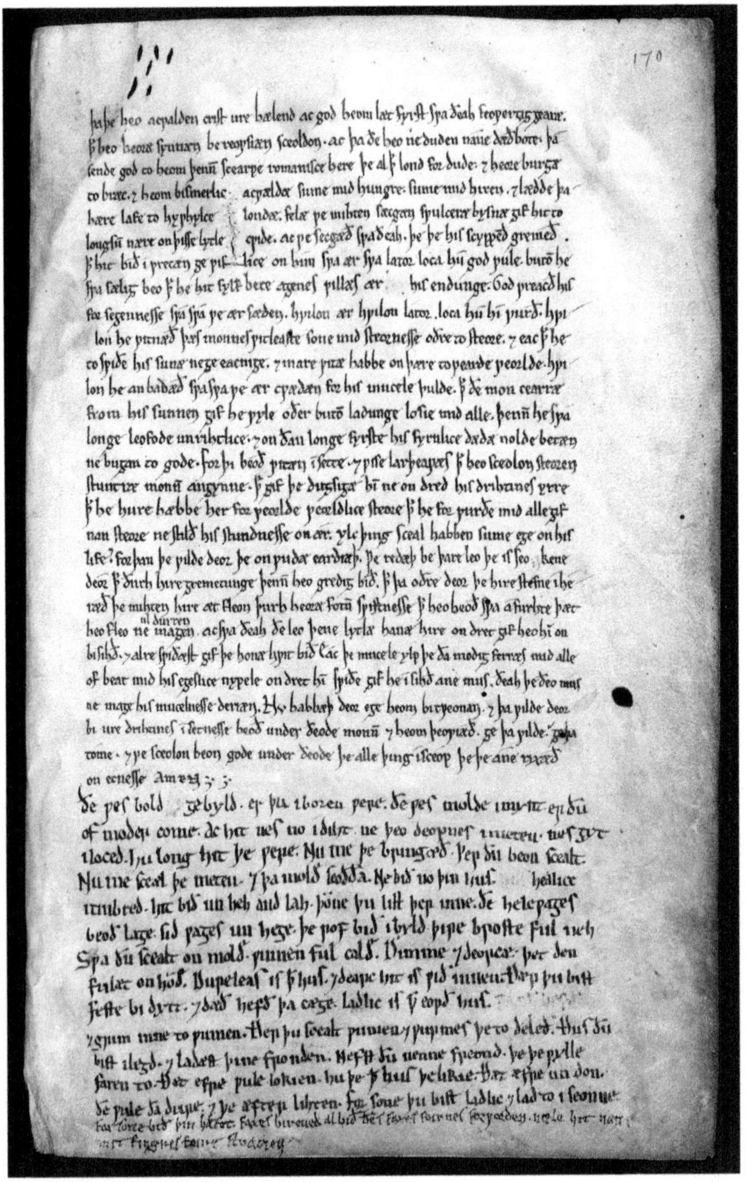

Fig. 1: Oxford, Bodleian Library, MS Bodley 343, fol 170r (photo: by permission of the Bodleian Library)

# Re-lining The Grave:
# A Slow Reading of MS Bodley 343, fol. 170r[1]

## CHRIS JONES

*For ET*
*on Remembrance Day, 11/11/2018*

*ðe wes bold gebyld*
For you a house was built.

We do not know who speaks to us. Or should I write: 'I do not know who speaks to me'? For that pronoun (*ðe*) seems singular, unless the second person had already begun the collapse of its distinction between number by the time of this utterance. (Unlikely. When was this utterance? *Patience. One problem at a time.*) I am sitting in my study staring at a digital image of a sentence which was inked onto the skin of a dead animal hundreds of years ago. Four words inside my four walls. It is dark. At this time of year the days close in quickly in Fife. The voice that addresses me is disembodied. If I practise patience, will it reveal itself? 'I' am an indirect object. Of the verb, but also of this verse. (*I believe these words a poem, but I cannot yet explain to you why.*) Apparently, I am the recipient of a house. Four walls in four words. Is their architect the same absentee who speaks

---

[1]    Oxford, Bodleian Library, Bodley 343, fol. 170r, lines 29 to 43. For description, see N.R. Ker, *Catalogue of Manuscripts Containing Anglo-Saxon* (Oxford: Clarendon Press, 1957), no. 301. For facsimile, see *Old English Verse Texts from Many Sources: A Comprehensive Edition*, ed. Fred C. Robinson and E.G. Stanley, Early English Manuscripts in Facsimile, XXIII (Copenhagen: Rosenkilde & Bagger, 1991), no. 36 (description on p. 27). For editions, see John Josias Conybeare, *Illustrations of Anglo-Saxon Poetry* (London: Harding & Lepard, 1826), 271–3 (missing last three lines); Benjamin Thorpe, ed., *Analecta Anglo-Saxonica: A selection in prose and verse from Anglo-Saxon authors of various ages*, rev. edn (London: John Russell Smith, 1868), 153–4; Richard Buchholz, ed., *Die Fragmente der Reden der Seele an den Leichnam in zwei Handschriften zur Worcester und Oxford* (Erlangen, 1890; rpt Amsterdam: Rodopi, 1970), 11; Arnold Schröer, 'The Grave', *Anglia* 5 (1882), 289–90; John W. Conlee, ed., *Middle English Debate Poetry: A critical anthology* (East Lansing: Colleagues Press, 1991), 4–5.

these words? Is this the builder? Saying that she has built for me?[2] I do
not know the builder's gender, so I will call her she. Of course, I believe
myself the addressee – these words are undoubtedly meant for me; that is
the conceit of reading and the egotism of being human. But this essay is
meant for you. Elaine. Catherine. Caroline. Reader. I shape these words
with you in mind. So from now on I will call *ðe* 'you'.

In the last paragraph I wrote 'house', yet the word *bold* is really 'building': *for you was a building built*. A tautology. Or an inevitability. How
else could a building be? Except by being built? Did you ask to be housed?
What did the speaker know, or presume to know, of you, of your life,
before she spoke? Before she built?

*ðe wes bold gebyld*
*er þu iboren were.*

For you was built a house
Before you were born.

Four more words. You were dative, but you have become nominative.
Then, an object, indirectly. Now, a subject. But a passive subject. The
speaker, or if not the speaker then at least the absent builder, built before
you were born. What could she possibly have known of you before your
birth? Of the kind of house in which you would wish to dwell? But you
are subordinate. Sequenced. You are a past event, one against which the
main clause is plotted; the building happened before your birth: the house
is older than your frame. You came after. You are not the main event. To
be blunt: you are not important, even when you are ostensibly the subject.

To be born is to have been carried for a full term; for someone to bear
you inside them, the walls of her womb their own kind of dwelling-place. She
bore you, and you were birthed by her. Your *birth*day is the day of her *bearing*
you. Bearing and building: the couplet presents them as equivalent, held in
a phonetic copula by the patterning of the three bilabial plosives. *Bold*, *byld*,
*bor*. Three beats. Of the hammer or heart. Three blows. Of heart or hammer.

*ðe wes molde imynt*

For you was earth meant

---

2    Conlee has written that it is uncertain whether the speaking voice is 'the
Soul addressing its Body, or a personified abstraction such as Death, or the mor-
alist-poet addressing an unspecified audience'. *Middle English Debate Poetry*, 3.

A third verse. Syntax the same as the first. Now you are again the object. Who intended earth for you? Or *the* earth? All of it? Or a handful? (*Patience.*) Perhaps the builder? Is this the material she chose for you? Earth, *molde*, rhymes with house, *bold*. Rhyme recalls sound that has passed. It is recuperative. It bids us not let the ephemeral vibrations in waves of air fade and disappear without trace. They are the materials of voice. The record of thought. Rhyme summons back vanished sounds to the ear's memory. Rhyme says: one comes after what came before. It is sameness, *old*; and difference, *b/m*. Likeness and unlike: a linked chain of simulacra and variants.

Rhyme marks endings as alliteration marks beginnings. A mesh of onset and offset. The textured gauze of speech. Yet *bold/molde* are not end rhymes in the technical sense of that phrase. They do not mark out the end of a 'line' of verse. They each nestle in the exact metrical midpoint of their three-stress (if we assign stress semantically) verses. But nor are they 'internal' rhymes, in the way in which we usually identify that device, as an echoing within a single line. Rather they call across to one another as next-door-but-one verses, a kind of medial interlace rhyme. Mirroring the subordinate clause of the second verse, a fourth verse names your mother, who was implicit, but not stated in that same second verse.

> ðe wes bold gebyld
> er þu iboren were.
> ðe wes molde imynt
> er ðu of moder come.

> For you a house was built
> Before you were born.
> For you the earth was meant
> Before you came from mother.

Syntactically, metrically, semantically, phonetically, the parallelism of the quatrain is almost too perfect. Each verse is in rising tripodic form ('iambic trimeter', to use anachronistic terminology for a moment: x / x / x /),[3] except that the first and third verses are both acephalous, creating a contrapuntal effect of seemingly falling on-verses delivering the main clauses, reversed with rising rhythm off-verses in the subordinate clauses.

---

[3]  NB, in the third verse I assume elision of the two unstressed vowels between *molde* and *imynt* into one, single dip.

*ac hit nes no idiht*
*ne þeo deopnes imeten*
*nes gyt iloced*
*hu long hit þe were.*

But it was not prepared,
Nor its depth measured,
Nor was it considered
How long it should be.

You must allow yourself to be baffled by the sheer oddness of these statements; after all, you have no title to guide you. How can a house be built before your birth if no measurements were taken, no preparations made? Why would a house be *deep* and long, not high? Houses are high. Or if not, then low, rather than *deep*. And their construction requires much careful measuring. Such paradoxes, and the puzzlement they cause you, are not dispelled as the disembodied voice continues:

*Nu me þe bringæð*
*þer ðu beon scealt.*
*Nu me sceal þe meten*
*& þa molde seoðða.*

Now you're brought
to where you have to be.
Now you're measured
and, afterwards, the earth.

I imagine you are taken aback by the force of that anaphoric *nu*. Now when? Now at the moment of reading? You thought you were merely reading these words, not being forcibly transported by an unnamed agency. Why are measurements only *now* being made, if the house were built before you existed? How were that, then possible? Where is the place you must be, if not here, in the moment of this very reading?

*Ne bið no þin hus*
*healice intinbred.*
*hit bið unheh and lah*
*þonne þu list þerinne.*

Nor is your house
built with high ceilings
It is unhigh and low
when you lie within it.

But houses are not 'unhigh'. The speaker is relentless in developing the oxymoronic idea of a *deop hus*. You find the privative particle attached to the adjective, 'un-', disturbing. It is not right. It should be enough to say 'low' if the speaker means 'low'. You are being promised a house made of deprivation, of qualities which are not.

> ðe helewages beoð lage
> sidwages unhege.
> þe rof bið ibyld
> þire broste ful neh.

> The gable walls are low,
> the side walls unhigh.
> The roof is built
> very near your breast.

Not high. Unhigh. Low. The walls. Low. The walls. Unhigh. The roof. Close. In their very repetitiousness the words enact oppression. They induce a sense of claustrophobia. There is a paucity of ideas and vocabulary in these statements, but that is not because of the speaker's poverty of articulation. Her obsessive reiteration of words and phrases reinforces the desperate poverty of the experience of living in this tiny space without relief or respite. You are feeling the first pangs of panic.

> swa ðu scealt on molde
> wunien ful calde.
> dimme & deorcæ
> þet den fulæt on honde.

> So you must live,
> stone cold in the earth.
> In dimness and darkness
> that den decays at your hands.[4]

By now you, who do not (*remember*) have the benefit of the title that scholars have chosen for these words, are beginning to suspect that despite all this talk of living and dwelling, in fact you are dying. Or perhaps you

---

[4]  I find this clause beyond my ability to translate satisfactorily. I am grateful to Elaine Treharne for helping me with the idiom *on hende*, which she taught me can mean: '"demanding attention", "on hand", "at hand", "nearby", "conveniently" but also "in (your) hands", or "in your possession", or even "around you".' Personal communication.

are already dead. What is death like? (*It is like living. After a fashion.*)
What kind of house is a house for the dead? How do the dead dwell? This
is the central conceit of the speaker's words, and, in a sense, she is asking
us a riddle. She says *hus*, but she does not mean *hus*. What, then, is to the
dead as a house to the living?

> *Dureleas is þæt hus*
> *& dearc hit is wiðinnen.*
> *Ðær þu bist feste bidytt*
> *& dæð hefð þa cæge.*

> Doorless is that house
> and dark it is within.
> There you are imprisoned
> and death has the key.

This does not make sense. If the house has no door, why is there a key?
(*Because the houses of the dead are like and unlike the houses of the living.*
*Death can let us in, but Death cannot let us out.*)

> *laðlic is þæt eorðhus*
> *& grim inne to wunien.*
> *Ðer þu scealt wunien*
> *& wurmes þe todeleð.*

> Terrible is that earth-house
> and it is grim to live there.
> There you must live
> and worms will share you.

Here is the central kenning underpinning the whole riddle: *eorðhus*.
What is to the whale as the road is to us? Which bird is to the halls of sky
as the poet is to the halls of humans? What is made in the ground that is
as a house to us? *For whom* is a house made, not on or over, but *in* and *of*
the earth? There has been much discussion of these words as belonging to
the medieval tradition of 'Body and Soul' literature, and that the speaker
could be a disembodied soul addressing her dead body.[5] This may well be
the case, but we might also learn to read these lines as belonging simultaneously to the long tradition of riddling. How is a shield like a chopping

---

5    Conlee, *Middle English Debate Poetry*, 3.

board?[6] A penis like kneaded dough? Or a house like the grave? This text explores these questions in frightening detail and these verses offer a few answers: like a normal house (*but terrible*). Dwelling there is like dwelling normally (*but without the comfort that dwelling means*). There is dining in that house (*but you are the meat*).

> Đus ðu bist ilegd
> & ladæst þine fronden.
> Nefst ðu nenne freond
> þe þe wylle faren to
> Đæt efre wule lokien
> hu þe þæt hus þe likie
> Đæt æfre undon
> ðe wule ða dure
> & þe æfter lihten.

> Thus you are laid,
> and you leave your friends.
> You'll never have a friend
> who will visit you,
> who will ever want to ask
> how you like that house,
> who will ever want
> to open that door
> and afterwards comfort you.

That this text explores in some depth (if you will forgive the pun), the metaphor of grave as house has been observed often before.[7] Moreover, it has also been noted that archaeological evidence seems to suggest that graves in Anglo-Saxon England were often built with vertical timber posts, to create chambers that were then roofed with timber planking and covered with earth.[8] For the readers and writers

---

[6]   That the solution to Old English 'Riddle 5' could, as well as 'shield', simultaneously be 'chopping board' also, was first proposed by Jennifer Neville: 'Joyous Play and Bitter Tears: The *Riddles* and the Elegies', in Richard North and Joe Allard, eds, *Beowulf and Other Stories: A new introduction to Old English, Old Icelandic and Anglo-Norman literatures* (Harlow: Pearson, 2007), 130–59. The other Exeter Book riddle I refer to here is number 45.

[7]   See Douglas D. Short, 'Aesthetics and Unpleasantness: Classical rhetoric in the medieval English lyric *The Grave*', *Studia Neophilologica* 48 (1976), 291–9 at 299, and Rosemary Woolf, *The English Religious Lyric in the Middle Ages* (Oxford: Oxford University Press, 1968), 83.

[8]   Douglas Moffat, 'The Grave in Early Middle English Verse: Metaphor and archaeology', *Florilegium* 6 (1984), 96–102.

of these words, the conceit of the grave as house was readily visible in the landscape in which they dwelled and died. What I wish to suggest here, however, is that the riddle tradition of early England often asks us to hold two 'solutions' in play simultaneously, without prioritising one as literal and other as metaphor, and to allow ourselves to wonder about the full ramifications of the conceit on both sides of the figure. (*If water is like a bone when it freezes, can my bones melt? If a worm devours words unthinkingly and can pupate into a moth, how do I consume words, and into what new growth do they propel me?*[9]) Similarly then, we need to think of these frightening pronouncements as not only imagining what death will be like, through the image of the grave as a kind of anti-house, but also causing us to reconsider our present dwelling as already in some ways like being dead. (*Are you not already imprisoned? Confined? Limited?*) To what extent are you, made of mould, both from and to dust, dying every day you are alive? It is a truism, but these words reframe that truism in appallingly vivid detail. Your body decays as it lives, its cells breaking down even as they attempt to renew. You wrinkle, you shrink, you turn grey.

> for sone þu bist ladlic
> & lad to iseonne.
> for sone bið þin hæfet
> faxes bireued.
> al bið ðes faxes
> feirnes forsceden.
> næle hit nan mit fingres
> feire stracien.

> For soon you are loathsome
> and horrific to be seen.
> For soon your head
> is bereft of hair.
> All the fairness
> of your hair is ravaged.
> No longer will it be stroked
> by fair fingers.

*** 

[9]  I allude here to riddles 69 and 47 respectively.

My first experience of a grave close up was after the funeral of my maternal grandmother Rosa Catherine. I was thirteen. I had visited her in the chapel of rest where she had looked (to me, surprisingly) just as I had known her. So much did she remind me of her former self, fallen asleep in the armchair of the back room in the afternoon sun, having left the peeled potatoes in a pan of water in the kitchen, the nicotine-streak of brown running upwards in a narrow line from her brow through her otherwise white, thinning hair, that I had dared myself to touch her hand one last time, but recoiled at the shock of its cold, clay-like lack of resistance to the impression my fingers made in her flesh. After the service, I found myself standing in a ring around the gaping hole of earth into which a team of black-suited strangers lowered Rosa's now-closed casket with considerable exertion into that dark maw. No-one had told me that the congregation would each shovel onto the lid of her coffin a small pile of the Welsh soil on which she had dwelled, and I was frightened when my turn came, unsure as to whether my age still excused me from such duties as a child, but also feeling a strong sense of obligation towards my grandmother, and that I ought now to 'be a man'. At the sound of that soil hitting the fast-disappearing wood a pit in my stomach opened. It came to my grandfather's turn last of all. Reginald Arthur, who had known loss and grief before. Whose first wife had died in his arms while he had been granted a few days' compassionate leave from the army. Who had known what it was to be locked up in close confinement. For almost five years a prisoner of war. Whose first child and only son had died of natural causes while he was hundreds of miles away. Who had poached rabbits and game illegally to keep his second family from hunger. Sewed nets for shrimp and second-hand clothes for thrift. Whom I had never seen cry. Who never talked of such things. Who laughed and teased and had thrown me over his shoulders when I was an infant. At the moment the shovel came to him I saw him collapse to his knees and, sobbing hysterically, try to climb down into the open grave. He threw himself so violently into the open hole that several family members had to restrain him and pull him back out from joining her there in that dark house. He was screaming *Rosie, Rosie, my Rosie*. His duck. It was the most frightening thing I had ever witnessed at that point in my life.

***

Such experiences are part of our reading. We pretend to dismiss them from the training that we put ourselves through as scholars of literature and of medieval history. They are 'subjective'. Personal. Emotive. They are all that, true. And they are also the tools with which we read, alongside palaeography, philology, prosody and theory. We do not respond to literature except by reference to such personal experiences. Yet we have largely banished such responses from our professional study of literature, in part out of understandable embarrassment at the lack of method or rigour for incorporating them with the other skills we have learned to practise. I will not be embarrassed at reading through my lived experience. Instead, I will found, with no small amount of self-irony, a new literary school, which I call here 'Personalism', and which I proclaim to be as important intellectually as historicism, both new and old, and all the host of other -isms of literary theory, even though I am quite confident that I will be its only ever disciple, and its only precept is 'You just go on your nerve.'[10]

This is a slow reading. It is slower than REF-cycles. The 'original contribution' I aim to make to the scholarship on this piece of literature is, shortly, to offer a new way of thinking about its formal structure, and in doing so to dismantle some of the editorial conventions that have grown up around it, and which I believe obscure our understanding of the way it does its dreadful work. But arriving at this understanding (which in any case is not as important to me as the emotional connection I have formed with these words) takes time. Time spent wondering, sometimes without purpose. Gazing into space. I have been slow-reading *The Grave* (for this is the title scholars have given these words) since I was thirteen years old. I have been practising for this moment, preparing myself for this reading, wishing to produce a small moment of closure in my relationship with it, just as every little ending and every little goodbye in our daily and weekly routines is a practice for the big goodbye. I hope to do it well, to read this poem with all the resources available to me, and to the best of my ability, not only because I love it deeply and am frightened deeply by it in equal measure, but also because (although I know this makes no rational sense three and a half decades later) I do not want to let down Reg and Rosa.

---

[10]   I do this in honour of Frank O'Hara, whose school of poetics 'Personism', announced in 1959, never attracted any followers, entirely as he anticipated. Frank O'Hara, 'Personism: A manifesto', repr. in *A Norton Anthology of Postmodern American Poetry*, ed. Paul Hoover (New York: W.W. Norton, 1994), 633–4. 'What can we expect of Personism? (This is getting good, isn't it?) Everything, but we won't get it. It is too new, too vital a movement to promise anything.' (p. 634).

So you must bear with me, just as Catherine Karkov, who is waiting patiently for this chapter, must bear with me a little more.[11] It is anachronistic to say I have been slow-reading *The Grave* since I was thirteen. At thirteen I would not encounter this poem for around another fifteen years, and I would not see it in its sole surviving manuscript copy (Fig. 1) for nine more years after that. Yet anachronism is what we do. To read medieval literature in 2018 with online searchable dictionaries produced by decades of labour by scholars with finely tuned philological sensitivities, with digital colour photographs of manuscript pages that can be enlarged many times over, with an edited corpus of other works, both later and earlier, with which we can compare a text like this for formal models and analogues, is anachronistic. Anachronism is inevitable in our work, and part of our method. To say I read this text through the trauma of watching my grandfather break down at the graveside of my grandmother, a twentieth-century sensibility read back over words composed by an individual almost a millennium ago, is not to argue that such readings are better or worse than those that try to recover something of the likely historical context for the individual who wrote these words; it is just what I happen to have to read with.

***

Anachronism, even if alleged only parenthetically (as I did when using the term 'iambic trimeter' a few pages ago), requires a sense of chronology for the charge to be permissible. And you have been patient; it is time to consider time. Ker wrote that the verses quoted above are in a hand that dates from the second half of the twelfth century, and no-one has disagreed with him since.[12] Of course, as with all medieval literature, to date the manuscript witness is not to date the composition of the work, which may

---

[11] This moment has gone now, of course. As has the moment when Caroline Palmer was waiting patiently for the revisions she generously suggested, one of which was that reference to this vanished moment be cut. But all moments are gone by the time of publication: the reference that follows to the anachronism of reading medieval texts in 2018 (it is now 2019, but will not be forever); the scribe's quivering performance of the poet's recollection of fine fingers caressing hair who knows how long after hair and fingers were long gone? It bears witness to a process, disavowing a state of finality, and all our readings are processes, not finalities.

[12] All kudos is due to Humphrey Wanley, who anticipated Ker's dating by around a century and a half when he judged the text to have been written about the time of the reign of Henry the Second.

well be earlier. Conybeare took it for granted that the words at the end
of folio 170r of MS Bodley 343 comprised a 'fragment of Anglo-Saxon
poetry' (although for Conybeare 'Anglo-Saxon' was a period category that
extended beyond 1066 and into the Norman period), and for him it was
'evident' that prosodically its words conformed to the metre 'universally
adopted by the Anglo-Saxon writers of verse'.[13] Robinson and Stanley's
inclusion of the poem in their *Old English Verse Texts* tacitly speaks of
their concurrence with Conybeare's view of the period to which these
verse belong, and of the poems with which they share a metrical affinity.
Conlee, on the other hand, speculates that the 'twenty-five alliterative
verses [...] may represent the earliest example of a Middle English poem
in the Body and Soul tradition', although he too believes that their form
'closely approximates the Anglo-Saxon alliterative line'.[14]

Here I should admit that I am sceptical as to whether it makes sense
to scan these verses, recorded approximately two centuries after the
poetry contained in the four major codices of Anglo-Saxon vernacular
poetry, as we do earlier, so-called 'classical' Old English poetry; if we
do, then I am aware that the four verses I quoted near the beginning of
this essay are all B-verses in Sieversian terminology (verses two and four
showing resolution in their final syllables): a repetition of rhythmical
verse-pattern that seems to have been eschewed in 'classical' Old English
poems.[15] But the repeated contrast between *ðe* and *ðu*, the addressee as

---

[13]   Conybeare, *Illustrations of Anglo-Saxon Poetry*, 270.

[14]   Conlee, *Middle English Debate Poetry*, 4. Incidentally, where Conlee here
speaks 'verses', I would say 'long lines'.

[15]   Eduard Sievers' 'five-types' analysis of Old English poetic metre was first set out
in 'Zur Rhythmik der germanischen Alliterationsverses', *Beiträge zur Geschichte der
deutschen Sprache und Literatur* 10 (1885), 209–314, 451–545; 12 (1887), 454–82.
Good, beginner-friendly summaries of the system can be found in Donald Scragg,
'The Nature of Old English Verse', in Malcom Godden and Michael Lapidge,
eds, *The Cambridge Companion to Old English Literature*, 2nd edn (Cambridge:
Cambridge University Press, 2013), 50–65, and in Bruce Mitchell and Fred C.
Robinson, *A Guide to Old English*, 8th edn (Oxford: Wiley-Blackwell, 2001), 143,
156–62. According to this system of scansion, B-verses are those that have two
'feet' (another anachronism) of rising rhythm (unstressed syllables followed by
a stressed syllable). Thus a B-verse can be equivalent to two iambs (dee-DUM,
dee-DUM), but in Old English poetry the first unstressed position could consist
of more than one unstressed syllable, so that an anapaest and an iamb would also
be equivalent to the Sieversian B-verse (diddy-DUM, dee-DUM). If one scans the
first four verses of *The Grave* according to this system, all have so-called 'expanded
dips' in their first position: verses 1 and 3 of two unstressed syllables (*ðe wes* in
both cases), and verses 2 and 4 of three unstressed syllables (*er þu i-* and *er ðu
of*). 'Resolution' just means that an unstressed syllable following (and part of the

object and as subject, seems to me so fundamental to the meaning of those lines that they demand pragmatic stress, and that this must be acknowledged by our scansion of these specific verses, if not our conception of the prosodic structure of the whole poem. By which I mean that a distinction might be made between the metre of the whole poem's *langue* and of its *parole* in the performance of individual verses, to speak in Saussurean terms.[16]

Assuming, for the moment then, a pragmatic performance of tripodic stress in those first four verses, it is the second, mid-stress of each verse that is the most important (and the first stress, if you do not accept tripodic scansion). An assonantal stream runs through the words in this position, alternating between two sets of interlaced rhyme and near-rhyme (*bold/mold-* and *-bor-/mod-*), which themselves differ only minimally in their vowel quality. Near end-rhyme occurs at the end of the first and third verses (the identical stressed vowel and final dental likeness of the participles *gebyld/imynt*). Not only do the nuclei of these words echo one another in their stem vowels and end-consonants in overlapping patterns, but the triple head-rhymes unite the verses in couplets, so that moulding and mothering are placed in phonetic balance with one another in a second couplet, just as building and bearing were made equivalent through alliteration in the first. In this way two symmetries bind the four verses together in mutually complementary ways: the alliteration into proximate or consecutive pairs; the rhymes and assonance into overlapping, or interlaced pairs.

---

same word as) a stressed syllable with a short vowel 'doesn't count' for metrical purposes. That is to say, resolution makes the *-e* of *were* and *come* disappear. A less faffy way of dealing with that final syllable in verses 2 and 4 might be to suggest that *were* and *come* could already be pronounced sometimes as monosyllables, and rather like Chaucer's final *-e*, need not be articulated when not required by metre. On the notion of 'classical' Old English, as a body of poems which this Sieversian system is fairly well suited to describe, as well as an attempt to modify Sievers so that other 'non-classical' Old English poems may also be described accurately, see Thomas A. Bredehoft, *Early English Metre* (Toronto: University of Toronto Press, 2005).

[16]     In his posthumous *Cours de linguistique générale* (1916), Saussure distinguished between language as an abstract system of rules and conventions that exists apart from any individual speakers (*langue*), and language as a specific utterance within (and from) that system (*parole*). *Parole* cannot exist without the context of *langue*, but the system of *langue* only comes about through cumulative instances of *parole*. But you already knew that, didn't you? (Caroline said I should put it in.) Ferdinand Saussure, *Course in General Linguistics*, trans. Wade Baskin, ed. Charles Bally and Albert Sechehaye, 3rd edn (New York: McGraw-Hill, 1966).

All this I need to labour, because I need to make the point that these verses are carefully laboured. As carefully as one timbers a house. Or digs a grave. If these verses, and those that follow them, are presumed to belong metrically to the tradition of Old English poetry, then in places they will be found to be irregular, defective even. They will be judged poorly built, still-born. I do not believe the maker of these symmetries did not know what she was making. In the syntactic, rhythmic and phonetic parallelism, these verses are too skilful for the poet who composed them to be incapable of knowing what she was doing elsewhere in her work.

***

I first saw MS Bodley 343 at first hand in April of 2008, when one still accessed the manuscripts of the Bodleian Library in the Duke Humfreys Reading Room. I sat that April in one of the narrow corridors running from the left of the central aisle, ending in one tall but narrow, draughty window, and lined high to the front and to the back with seventeenth-century bookshelves that obscured others' view of me. A narrow, dark, confined space. I had been through a bad break-up two years previously, and was still 'doing a lot of work' in the language of the self-help books, to process the sense of grief I had experienced, and to overcome the sense of narcissism with which one can imprison oneself after a bad break-up. We had met, on several occasions, elsewhere in that library, on and off, over the course of three years. I sat and stared into space, wondering without purpose, remembering, and reading slowly, as the manuscript hand forced me to do, thinking of fingers not stroking hair any longer. My own personal life provided a context for my reading, as it must. My story framed the way I understood the poem, and the poem framed the way I understood my story. Sometimes it can be good to have to come to terms with giving up what one does not wish to give up. It teaches us the selfishness and the futility of our desires. To practise for the big goodbye. In April 2008 Bodley 343 fol. 170r taught me such humilities.

***

Occupying fourteen manuscript lines of manuscript space, and filling the remainder of a recto left after the completion of the previous item in Bodley 343, Ælfric's Homily for the Common of a Confessor,[17] the

---

[17] The bulk of the manuscript is comprised of homilies, mainly by Ælfric, although also by Wulfstan and anonymous authors, together with a few other

verses of this poem are written out continuously across the full width
of the writing space, as was the convention for vernacular poetry in this
period. Yet these verses are also almost all uniformly marked off from
one another by punctuation marks, suggesting that the '*langue*' prosodic
structure of the whole piece consists of units of four metrical positions,
each comprising two lifts and two dips (with some examples of anacrusis).
Indeed, no punctuation marks occur in positions other than those which
coincide with such two-stress verse units, reinforcing the likelihood that
the pointing is metrical.

In addition to the points that Schröer records in his edition, I also see
*punctus* marks in the manuscript in three other places which he misses (all
at the 'mid-line caesura' as he sets them out, though I find such terminology unhelpful in thinking about the form of this poem), that is: after *hus*
(line 7a in his lineation); after *ibyld* (his 10a); after *wunien* (his 16a).[18] I
also read the mark after *deorcæ* (12a) as a *punctus elevatus*, although I have
no explanation for this, a mark seemingly unique within the text of the
poem. In fact, the only verse end-boundary which seems to be unpunctu-
ated in the first thirteen manuscript lines of the text (the last two lines
are a special case, discussed below) is 10b, after *neh*, which occurs at the
end of a manuscript line (manuscript line 34) and is followed in the next
manuscript line by one of three larger capitals, which are also set slightly
further to the left than the regular left-hand margin of most of the text
block (*Ð* in the opening manuscript line of the poem, or line 29 of the
whole page; *N* in manuscript line 32; and *S* in manuscript line 35). Both
these conditions are also true of the verse ending with *scealt*, however, at
the end of manuscript line 31, yet this is clearly pointed nonetheless. All
of which is to say that the metrical punctuation is, with the one exception
of Schröer's 'half-line' 10b, remarkably consistent, much more so, in fact,
than the manuscripts of many earlier English poetic texts:[19]

items in both Latin and the vernacular, and three examples of musical notation.
For a full description of Bodley 343's contents, see its entry in the superlative
'Production and Use of English Manuscripts 1060–1220': https://www.manu-
scriptsonline.org/resources/pu/ (accessed 8 June 2019).

[18]   Conlee avoids having to commit himself to these marks, by leaving them all
out in his edition; arguably for him they are in any case redundant, given that he
uses lineation and caesura to indicate verse boundaries.

[19]   My transcription modernises all insular characters except thorn and eth, and
expands abbreviations with italics, except for Tironian 'and', which it replaces
with ampersand. I have not here changed word boundaries, so that *unheh* and
*perinne* (manuscript line 33), *sidwages* and *unhege* (ms line 34), *wiðinnen* (ms
line 36), *bidytt* and *eorðhus*, which I take to be a compound (ms line 37), *todeleð*

Ðe wes bold gebyld . er þu iboren were. ðe wes molde imynt . er ðu
of moder come. ac hit nes no idiht . ne þeo deopnes imeten . nes gyt
iloced . hu long hit þe were . Nu me þe bringæð . þer ðu beon scealt .
Nu me sceal þe meten . & þa molde seoðða . Ne bið no þin hus . healice
intinbred . hit bið un heh and lah . þonne þu list þer inne . ðe helewages
beoð lage. sid wages un hege . þe rof bið ibyld . þire broste ful neh
Swa ðu scealt on molde . wunien ful calde . Dimme & deorcæ ; þet den
fulæt on honde . Dureleas is þæt hus . & dearc hit is wið innen . Ðær þu bist
feste bi dytt . & dæð hefð þa cæge . laðlic is þæt eorð hus .
& grim inne to wunien . Ðer þu scealt wunien. & wurmes þe to deleð . Ðus ðu
bist ilegd . & ladæst þine fronden . Nefst ðu nenne freond . þe þe wylle
faren to . Ðæt efre wule lokien . hu þe þæt hus þe likie . Ðæt æfre un don .
ðe wule ða dure . & þe æfter lihten . for sone þu bist ladlic . & lad to i seonne .
for sone bið þin hæfet . faxes bireued. al bið ðes faxes feirnes forsceden . næle hit nan
mit fingres feire stracien

Here it is necessary also to note that the last two manuscript lines
(42 & 43) are in a different ductus from the rest of the poem (29 to
41), appearing lighter and shakier than the preceding lines. This has
caused several scholars, from Ker onwards, to pronounce these last two
lines (and six verses) as written in a later, probably early thirteenth-
century hand, and so possibly not original to the poem's composition.[20]
Robinson and Stanley, on the other hand, have argued that 'the last
three [long verse] lines could be in the same hand as the rest of the
poem, the difference in general appearance of the writing being because
it was executed at the bottom of the page where there was no place for
the writing hand to rest'.[21] In principle, this could indeed be a cause
for the apparent difference, although after careful deliberation I am
persuaded enough that differences in the formation of some characters
in the last two manuscript lines are more suggestive of a new hand (for

(ms line 38), *undon* (ms line 40) and *iseonne* (ms line 41) are each given with the
word division as it appears in the manuscript. My transcription does not show
three erasure gaps: between *bold* and *gebyld* (ms line 29, a gap of probably two
characters); between *hus* and *healice* (ms line 32, a gap of three or four characters,
starting *h* and so probably a mistake for *healice*); after *hus* at the end of ms line 37
(appearing to start with Tironian 'and'). NB my transcription, in agreement with
Conlee, but against Schröer, reads *laðlic* in ms line 37. The crossbar through the
eth's ascender is very faint, but in comparison with *ladlic* (ms line 41), I believe
it is there.

20    Conlee, for example, relegates these lines to a footnote on these grounds.
*Middle English Debate Poetry*, 56.
21    *Old English Texts from Many Sources*, 27.

example, the cross bars in the eth of the last two lines are more assertive, starting further to the left than in the earlier lines, and lacking the
curve in the downward flourish of the right of the cross bar, and the
minims of the 'n' in the final lines are also more angular, less curved). In
these last two lines there are metrical points lacking in two places where
we might have expected them on the basis of the preceding lines (after
*faxes*, and after *fingres*), suggesting that this latter scribe had different
expectations from the first as to the reader's competency in detecting
verse boundaries.

As the first scribe has given us such guidance with verse boundaries, it
is possible to lineate this poem, and all previous editors do so, according
to the editorial conventions for Old English poetry, assuming alliterative
pair-bonded verses in long lines with a caesura to be the norm:

Ðe wes bold gebyld . er þu iboren were.
ðe wes molde imynt . er ðu of moder come.
ac hit nes no idiht . ne þeo deopnes imeten .
nes gyt iloced . hu long hit þe were .
Nu me þe bringæð . þer ðu beon scealt .                5
Nu me sceal þe meten . & þa molde seoðða .
Ne bið no þin hus . healice intinbred .
hit bið unheh and lah . þonne þu list þerinne .
ðe helewages beoð lage. sidwages unhege .
þe rof bið ibyld . þire broste ful neh                10
Swa ðu scealt on molde . wunien ful calde .
Dimme & deorcæ ; þet den fulæt on honde .
Dureleas is þæt hus . & dearc hit is wiðinnen .
Ðær þu bist feste bidytt . & dæð hefð þa cæge .
laðlic is þæt eorðhus . & grim inne to wunien .        15
Ðer þu scealt wunien. & wurmes þe todeleð .
Ðus ðu bist ilegd . & ladæst þine fronden .
Nefst ðu nenne freond . þe þe wylle faren to .
Ðæt efre wule lokien . hu þe þæt hus þe likie .
Ðæt æfre undon . ðe wule ða dure .                    20
        & þe æfter lihten .
for sone þu bist ladlic . & lad to iseonne .
for sone bið þin hæfet . faxes bireued.
al bið ðes faxes      feirnes forsceden .
næle hit nan mit fingres      feire stracien[22]       25

---

[22]   Here I have modernised the word boundaries of those compounds noted in
the footnote to my initial transcription.

Immediately we notice a problem that was not apparent in the manuscript lineation: a gap. Two does not go into forty-nine verses, and if we assume alliterative pair-bonding, that means something is missing. There is a hole in our grave. Both Schröer and Conlee assume that the widowed verse to be 21b (poem lineation, not manuscript), although nothing is lacking in sense, and given their assumptions about the structure of the poem I do not see why the gap could not actually occur at 21b (instead of at a missing 21a), or indeed at either 22a or 22b: *& þe æfter lihten* could be pair-bonded with *for sone þu bist ladlic*; this would cause alliteration to fall on the fourth lift of a relineated line 21, which is not permitted in 'classical' Old English verse by our current understanding of its conventions, but which is already required to make sense of the pair-bonding of lines 18 and 19 of this interpretation of the poem's structure (which is, in any case recorded much later than the bulk of 'Old English' verse):[23]

> Ðæt æfre undon . ðe wule ða dure .          20
> & þe æfter lihten . for sone þu bist ladlic .
> & lad to iseonne .
> for sone bið þin hæfet . faxes bireued.

Yet other problems present themselves if we attempt to understand the poem's structure in this way. Conlee notes that lines 11 and 15 of this editorial interpretation 'fail' to alliterate, although he suggests that 11 might be thought redeemed by an intended rhyme between *molde* and *calde*. Moreover, if we accept the 'additional' six verses as part of our text, line 23 also lacks alliteration, and in several other places the poem appears to indulge in fourth-stress alliteration, not only to justify the bond between verses in lines 18 and 19, as noted above, but also 'accidentally' at lines 6, 9, 22 and 24.[24]

As I was at pains to point out earlier in this essay, on the evidence of the opening verses our poet is a master of lyric patterning. Rather than adopt a language of lacks, gaps and failings then, as a result of assumptions about structural conventions I am scarcely able to justify on grounds of literary genre or period, I would rather give up those assumptions. Few of these 'problem' lines, according to the Schröer–Conlee editorial tradition,

---

[23]   Line 9 might also be thought to rely on alliteration on the fourth lift, if *hege* is interpreted as that lift, rather than *un*, from which, as we noted earlier it is separated by the scribe's word division.

[24]   I doubt that the prohibition on fourth-stress alliteration was universal to all genres of Old English poetry: it occurs in a number of the riddles in the Exeter Anthology.

are entirely devoid of phonetic or rhetorical echoes of their neighbouring verses. As Conlee notes, verse-end rhyme was likely thought suitable equivalence to alliteration in his line 11, rather as Brehe argues for his relineation of *The First Worcester Fragment*, by analogy with a number of the lines in Layamon's *Brut* that also employ 'internal' rhyme at the verse-end boundaries.[25]

As we saw earlier, our poet deliberately used rhyme in the early verses of her poem, although *bold* and *molde* do not mark verse-end boundaries, and like the half-rhymes of *gebyld* and *imynt*, they are not internal to the long line (as this editorial tradition conceives the poem), but rather produce a kind of couplet rhyme in the a-verses of this long line, although that is a rather inelegant way of describing quite an elegant echoic structure. Nevertheless, these examples lend weight to the assumption that our poet weaves deliberate patterns between verses by using rhyme as well as alliteration. Moreover, if we are to take this poem as this essay started to discuss it, verse by verse, instead of 'line' by 'line', then not only are we able to describe these rhymes more sensibly, as 'overlapping' or 'interlace', but we can note far more relationships of proximate verse patterning than our description based on pair-bonding into 'long lines' would easily accommodate:

> Ðe wes bold gebyld .
> er þu iboren were.
> ðe wes molde imynt .
> er ðu of moder come.
> ac hit nes no idiht .                    5
> ne þeo deopnes imeten .
> nes gyt iloced .
> hu long hit þe were .
> Nu me þe bringæð .
> þer ðu beon scealt .                    10
> Nu me sceal þe meten .
> & þa mold*e* seoððа .
> Ne bið no þin hus .
> healice intinbred .
> 15 hit bið unheh and lah .
> þon*n*e þu list þerinne .
> ðe helewages beoð lage.
> sidwages unhege .

[25]   S.K. Brehe, 'Reassembling the First Worcester Fragment', *Speculum* 65 (1990), 521–36.

þe rof bið ibyld .
þire broste ful neh                          20
Swa ðu scealt on molde .
wunien ful calde .
Dimme & deorcæ ;
þet den fulæt on honde .
Dureleas is þæt hus .                        25
& dearc hit is wiðinnen .
Ðær þu bist feste bidytt .
& dæð hefð þa cæge .
laðlic is þæt eorðhus .
& grim inne to wunien .                      30
Ðer þu scealt wunien.
& wurmes þe todeleð .
Ðus ðu bist ilegd .
& ladæst þine fronden .
Nefst ðu nenne freond .                      35
þe þe wylle faren to .
Ðæt efre wule lokien .
hu þe þæt hus þe likie .
Ðæt æfre undon .
ðe wule ða dure .                            40
& þe æfter lihten .
for sone þu bist ladlic .
& lad to iseonne .
for sone bið þin hæfet .
faxes bireued.                               45
al bið ðes faxes
feirnes forsceden .
næle hit nan mit fingres
feire stracien

Immediately, we can note that Schröer and Conlee's widowed line
21b can now be seen as inaugurating a triple-verse 'run' alliterating on /l/
(new lines 41–43), but that this in turn overlaps with another triple-verse
'run' alliterating on /s/ (new lines 42–44) where the central two verses
comprising this pair of interlinked alliterative triples (new lines 42–43)
contain both alliterators, /s/ and /l/, in a 'chiasmic' structure (I slightly
regret using that word here, as I think it tends to imply looking at words,
rather than hearing them) of: S L / L S, in envelope fashion, and where
the first S alliterator (*sone*) most surely have been heard as either a full
or very near full rhyme with the second, in the next verse (-*Seonne*: an
independent lexeme in the scribe's word division, remember). At the same

time, the second /l/ alliterator in this triple-run, and the first in the central 'envelope' couplet, *lad-*, rhymes fully with the third /l/ (second /l/ in the central envelope), *lad* (also new lines 42–43). In full, this complex pattern works something like the following:

- line 41 – opens /l/ alliteration
- line 42 – opens S alliteration with S rhyme; continues L alliteration & introduces L rhyme
- line 43 – continues L alliteration & completes L rhyme; continues S alliteration & S rhyme
- line 44 – completes S alliteration with S rhyme

There is no reason to think of there being any 'gap' in the verse structure here at all. Moreover, we should note that this 'new' line 44 (from now on, all numbers refer to the single-verse lineation I have just offered the reader unless otherwise noted) is actually in the second, later hand, and not only completes the full, double envelope pattern started by the three preceding verses in the earlier hand, but also produces a full example of interlaced anaphora by echoing the *for sone* of its ante-preceding verse. If these last six verses are not original to the composition of lines 1–43, then they are newly composed with a craftswomanly understanding of the structure of the foregoing lines, and a skilful ability to act out that understanding in fresh composition.

Other patterns of alliterative conjoining, in sequences longer than pair-bonds are in fact relatively common in this lyric masterpiece. Lines 13–15 all alliterate on /h/, for example, with line 15 not only completing the triple-verse /h/ pattern, but also introducing /l/, which will become the new alliterator for the next three verse. In this way we could hear line 15 as a pivot-verse participating in two overlapping alliterative runs of three verses (13 to 15, on /h/, and also 15 to 17 on /l/), but where the final line in the second triple run (line 17) also reintroduces /h/ from the first triple run, so that it seems to 'sum up' both of the key head-rhymes of the previous four verses. Line 17's /h/ is then reprised one more time in line 18, couplet fashion, a phonetic relationship further intensified by the fact that the subsequent elements of the compound words whose opening syllables form the first two lifts in lines 17 and 18 (*hel-* and *sid-*) are full rhymes (*-wages*: these two compounds perhaps most nearly shaping the metre of their verses to approximately that of the E-types of the Sieversian system of classifying Old English verse forms). Moreover, they are near-as-damn-it full rhymes with the second lift of line 17, *lage*, which in turn is as close a rhyme with the second lift of as its following verse (*hege*) as

were *molde* and *calde* in Conlee's old line number 11, and likely also close
rhymes echoing *heh* and *lah* of new line 15, and anticipating the upcom-
ing *neh* of line 20. In short, verses 13 to 20 exhibit an extremely densely
patterned weave of both overlapping and proximate rhymes, half-rhymes
and alliterations, that numbering in long lines (7 to 10) with the expec-
tation of finding simple pairs of alliterative bonds, can scarcely describe
with full justice.

Similarly, long runs of alliterators take place across new lines 23 to
28 (six verses of /d/, which also envelope an /h/ couplet at 24 and 25).
A triple /w/ runs from lines 31 to 33. Two non-consecutive /l/ couplets
(lines 33–34 and 37–38) envelope and overlap a triple run of second-
lift /f/ alliterators (lines 34–36) and a /w/ couplet (36–37), bringing us
only two verses away from the effect previously described for lines 41–44,
which also involves /l/ alliteration, so that we might think of lines 33 to
44 as forming one long, complex overlapping series of patterns in which
/l/ is the key repeated phoneme. Finally, lines 44 and 45 seem to me
likely bound in the near-rhyme of their final assonance and consonance,
in *hæfet/-reued*, the second verse of which pair also inaugurates a five-verse
run of /f/ alliterators with double deployment of rhyme riche in both
chiasmatic and interlace patterns (*faxes*, the first lift of 45 and the second
of 46, and *feir-*, the first lift of lines 47 and 49).

Two consequences follow from relineating *The Grave* according to this
principle. Firstly, and in a local sense more trivially (although it may be of
importance for how we conceive of late Old English/early Middle English
verse more generally), we no longer need to indulge in special pleading
to explain 'fourth-stress' alliteration. We need no longer do this, because
there are no longer four-stress 'long-lines' in which such alliterators seem
to break the rules of *Beowulf* and other 'classical' Old English poems.
Lines 18–19 in the Schröer–Conlee editorial structuring are no longer
problematic in this respect as 'new' lines 35–38, where, as we have already
seen, they participate in longer patterns that start at verse 33 and end at
verse 44. In such long and complex sequences of multiple overlapping
phonetic patterns, it is pointless to try to condition the ear to hear binary
pairs of *a*- and *b*- verses in which the key alliterator falls on the 'head-
stave' lift of a *b*-verse. Indeed, we no longer need to describe fourth-stress
alliteration as 'accidental' in old line numbers 6, 9, 22 and 24. In new
verse 12, the /s/ alliteration is a crucial part of an envelope pattern of S
M / M S, formed together with verse 11. The fundamental lynch-pin role
that verse 18's second lift of *hege* plays with its neighbouring verses has
already been described, as has that of verse 43 and 47. Indeed, freed from
the assumptions of 'long-line' lineation, all these 'decorative' examples of

alliterative embellishment are seen as the structurally crucial elements of a more flexible, open verse form that they really are.

Secondly, and perhaps of more importance to our immediate literary critical response to this extraordinary piece (if less significant to our conceptualisation of the expectations made of poems in this period): none of these verses are widowed. There are no holes in our grave. Every single verse line participates in one or more phonetic bonds with one or more of its neighbouring verses at a distance of no more than two verses. *The Grave* does not lack. Is not flawed. Does not fail at things it does not set itself to succeed at. Does not want what it cannot have. It is self-assured. Sturdily *intinbred*. Skilfully measured, metred, *imeten*.

\*\*\*

What kind of reader did its poet want us to be then? She wanted us not to put her poem into mated pair-bonds, for she did not conceive it so, and if we do, then we cannot hear (or more to the point, since most of us now are more visual readers than we are aural readers, we cannot readily *see*) the longer chains of phonetic association with which the poem links us from beginnings to endings, from being born to being buried, the callbacks to verses that are further than those merely proximate. She imagined and effected connections that were more than merely binary. She wrote in a fluid and flexible open-structure, a form not symmetrically regular, but not disordered either. One in which meaning and pattern surprise us, precisely because it does not come at points ordered regularly and expected, but with some of the spontaneity and sense of contingency that is our lived experience. She was a masterful poet, and so she hoped we would be masterful readers. Which, if we are to live up to her expectations, must mean to read slowly.

\*\*\*

I was twenty-six years old when my father buried his father, Wallace Llewellyn, then my last living grandparent, in the Welsh soil on which he and his forefathers and foremothers had dwelled. I was exactly twice the age as I was when we buried Rosa Catherine, the first of my four grandparents to die. Half my life then to know all four, half my life then to lose all four. If Ker is right about date of the hand that wrote the first verses of *The Grave*, and if we assume on average around twenty-five years between generations, then at that moment there were approximately 32 generations between me and the person who wrote those verses, and which I would soon be studying. Having known family members to the fourth generation back from my own, my own horizon of memory was then therefore about an eighth of the total distance in time back to the scribe's life. At the time of Llew's funeral, my father, Richard Llewellyn, was experiencing multiple kinds of grief, still dealing, as he was, with his own bad break-up, my mother, Lynne Dianne, having left him two years earlier. Another broken pair. Yet he spoke during the service, and although I cannot now recall all that he said, I remember he concluded by drawing a sheet of paper from his pocket. Then, over the coffin of his father, eyes brimming but somehow not actually crying, he fixed by turns first my face, and then that of my brother Matthew Iain, and read *slowly*, in a voice wavering but clear, holding our gaze as his did so, a passage from Llew's favourite novel, Richard Llewellyn's *How Green was My Valley*:

> I saw behind me those who had gone, and before me, those who are to come. I looked back and saw my father, and his father, and all our fathers, and in front, to see my son, and his son, and the sons upon sons beyond.
>
> And their eyes were my eyes.
>
> As I felt, so they had felt, and were to feel, as then, so now, as tomorrow and forever. Then I was not afraid, for I was in a long line that had no beginning, and no end, and the hand of his father grasped my father's hand, and his hand was in mine, and my unborn son took my right hand, and all, up and down the line stretched from Time That Was, to Time That Is, and is not yet, raised their hands to show the link, and we found that we were one, born of Woman, Son of Man, had in the Image, fashioned in the Womb by the Will of God, the eternal Father.
>
> I was one of them, they were of me, and in me, and I in all of them.[26]

***

| | |
|---|---|
| Ðe wes bold gebyld | For you a house was built, |
| er þu iboren were | before you were born. |
| ðe wes molde imynt | For you the earth was meant, |
| er ðu of moder come | before you came from mother. |
| ac hit nes no idiht | But it was not prepared,                 5 |

---

[26]  Richard Llewellyn, *How Green Was My Valley* (London: Penguin, 2001), 273.

| | |
|---|---|
| ne þeo deopnes imeten | nor its depth measured, |
| nes gyt iloced | nor was it considered |
| hu long hit þe were | how long it should be. |
| Nu me þe bringæð | Now you're brought |
| þer ðu beon scealt | to where you have to be. 10 |
| Nu me sceal þe meten | Now you're measured |
| & þa molde seoðða | and, afterwards, the earth. |
| Ne bið no þin hus | Nor is your house |
| healice intinbred | built with high ceilings. |
| hit bið unheh and lah | It is unhigh and low 15 |
| þonne þu list þerinne | when you lie within it. |
| ðe helewages beoð lage | The gable walls are low, |
| sidwages unhege | the side walls unhigh. |
| þe rof bið ibyld | The roof is built |
| þire broste ful neh | very near your breast. 20 |
| Swa ðu scealt on molde | So you must live, |
| wunien ful calde | stone cold in the earth. |
| Dimme & deorcæ | In dimness and darkness |
| þet den fulæt on honde | that den decays at your hands. |
| Dureleas is þæt hus | Doorless is that house 25 |
| & dearc hit is wiðinnen | and dark it is within. |
| Ðær þu bist feste bidytt | There you are imprisoned |
| & dæð hefð þa cæge | and death has the key. |
| laðlic is þæt eorðhus | Terrible is that earth-house |
| & grim inne to wunien | and it is grim to live there. 30 |
| Ðer þu scealt wunien | There you must live |
| & wurmes þe todeleð | and worms will share you. |
| Ðus ðu bist ilegd | Thus you are laid, |
| & ladæst þine fronden | and you leave your friends. |
| Nefst ðu nenne freond | You'll never have a friend 35 |
| þe þe wylle faren to | who will visit you, |
| Ðæt efre wule lokien | who will ever want to ask |
| hu þe þæt hus þe likie | how you like that house, |
| Ðæt æfre undon | who will ever want |
| ðe wule ða dure | to open that door 40 |
| & þe æfter lihten | and afterwards comfort you. |
| for sone þu bist ladlic | For soon you are loathsome |
| & lad to iseonne | and horrifying to be seen. |
| for sone bið þin hæfet | For soon your head |
| faxes bireued | is bereft of hair. 45 |
| al bið ðes faxes | All the fairness |
| feirnes forsceden | of your hair is ravaged. |
| næle hit nan mit fingres | No longer will it be stroked |
| feire stracien | by fair fingers. |

Slow Looking

# Rethinking Slow Looking:
## Encounters with Clonmacnoise[1]

### HEATHER PULLIAM

Although careful looking has always been an essential aspect of art historical practice,[2] over the past ten years it has transformed from an embedded methodology to a movement and *cause célèbre*. Slow Art Day was
launched in 2009, occurring in sixteen museums worldwide. By 2018,
over 1,200 events had taken place across the world.[3] In New York, the
Museum of Modern Art is hosting Quiet Mornings that end with meditation sessions. The museum's website urges participants to 'look slowly. …
Enjoy the serenity of being surrounded by Claude Monet's monumental
*Water Lilies*, find space for personal reflection in the minimalist canvases
of Agnes Martin.'[4] In London, Tate Modern is planning slow looking
sessions for its 2019 Pierre Bonnard exhibition.[5] A variety of British and
American newspapers, the BBC, and NPR have all featured articles that
explain and advocate slow looking.[6] Lectures at Oxford and Harvard uni-

[1]  The research leading to this essay was supported by the Leverhulme Trust
as part of a research fellowship, 'From 2D to 4D: Ireland's Medieval Crosses in
Time, Motion and the Environment'. I am grateful to the Clonmacnoise Office
of Public Works staff for all of their assistance on-site.
[2]  For a brief consideration of slow looking as part of art historical practice in
the nineteenth and twentieth centuries, see David M. Lubin, 'Slow Looking',
*A History of Art at Oxford University* (blog), 26 July 2017, https://oxfordarthist.
wordpress.com/2017/07/26/slow-looking/ (accessed 5 November 2018).
[3]  http://www.slowartday.com/about/ (accessed 5 November 2018).
[4]  https://www.moma.org/calendar/programs/77 (accessed 5 November 2018).
[5]  https://www.theguardian.com/artanddesign/2018/jul/23/tate-modern-slow
-looking-pierre-bonnard-exhibition-2019 (accessed 5 November 2018).
[6]  For example, see Oliver Burkeman 'Why Patience Really is a Virtue', *The
Guardian*, 21 August 2015, https://www.theguardian.com/artanddesign/short-
cuts/2018/jul/24/why-taking-it-slow-in-an-art-gallery-could-change-your-life;
Stephanie Rosenbloom, 'The Art of Slowing Down in a Museum', *The New
York Times,* 9 October 2014, https://www.nytimes.com/2014/10/12/travel/the-
art-of-slowing-down-in-a-museum.html; Terry Teachout, 'How Seeing Less Is
More', *The Wall Street Journal*, 3 April 2017; Linda Kennedy, 'How to Look
at a Work of Art', *BBC Culture*, 24 March 2017, http://www.bbc.com/culture/
story/20170324-how-to-look-at-a-work-of-art; 'Can Slow-Moving Art Disrupt

versities have focused upon the practice, and art history courses across the UK and the US have assigned slow looking exercises for students.[7] Interest and support for the movement have primarily come from organisations, people and events that serve as conduits between art's public and academic spheres: museums, the media and educators.

This essay probes certain assumptions inherent within the recent discussions of slow looking. These include implicit binaries lodged within the approach, particularly within the contexts of the physical and the virtual. It will also consider how slow looking applies to early medieval monuments and, conversely, how we might both broaden and refine the concept of slow looking in response to the nature of these objects and their viewers, both past and present. Except for a book by Arden Reed discussed below, the main platforms for the slow looking movement have been newspapers, broadcasts, podcasts, blogs, lectures and a single textbook. Although written by academics, curators and art critics, the focus has primarily been pedagogical and not necessarily aimed at scholarly audiences. Similarly, this essay does not intend to offer an academic analysis of the high crosses of Clonmacnoise but rather to rethink the methodologies of the slow looking movement, their suitability to medieval material, and intersections with other approaches such as phenomenology. In this, the high crosses serve as an occasional sounding board, although some new avenues of research and preliminary conclusions are presented.

Like slow cooking, the slow looking movement emerged as a reaction to the speed of modern life. Supporters most commonly cite viewing practices within galleries as the instigator for the movement, frequently referring to the findings of a 2001 study at the Metropolitan Museum of Art, which demonstrated that visitors spent a median of 17 seconds in front

Our Hectic Routines?', *NPR TED Radio Hour*, 26 August 2016, https://www.npr.org/2016/08/26/490627461/can-slow-moving-art-disrupt-our-hectic-routines?t=1542016598132 (all accessed 5 November 2018); Shari Tishman, *Slow Looking: The art and practice of learning through observation* (London: Routledge, 2017); see also footnote below.
7    Lubin, 'Slow Looking'; Jennifer Roberts, 'Slow Looking', paper presented at Harvard Initiative for Learning and Teaching Conference 2013, https://www.youtube.com/watch?v=AnQVT_p6pxg (accessed 5 November 2018); for examples of undergraduate assignments, see Maggie Williams et al., 'Slow Down!', *Material Collective* (blog), 19 December 2017, http://thematerialcollective.org/slow-down/; Angela Bennett Segler, 'Slow Knowing II: The Metropolitan Museum of Art', *Mental Sphere* (blog), 3 December 2013.

of individual paintings.[8] Most advocates are quick to assert that they do not reject digital technologies but merely wish to explore and make use of slow looking as one of many, equally viable tools for the exploration and study of art. It is clear, however, that slow looking is not merely a general response to the frantic pace of modern life but rather more specifically to the impact of digital technologies on viewing practice. Arden Reed writes, 'Americans spend between six to ten seconds looking at individual works in museums. (Is it just a coincidence that six to ten seconds is also the average time browsers perch on any given Web page)?'[9] The most consistent feature within these discussions of slow looking is the insistence that audiences 'turn off their smartphones and close their laptops' and go to view works of art in the flesh.[10] In the 2013 article that provoked much of the recent interest in slow looking, Jennifer Roberts argued that 'every external pressure, social and technological, is pushing students in the other direction, toward immediacy, rapidity, and spontaneity' and that students needed to be encouraged to 'learn in a visceral way'.[11]

On the whole, discussions of slow looking suggest two modes of viewing that are in opposition to one another, generating the kinds of binaries summarised in the table:

| Slow | Fast |
| --- | --- |
| Physical | Virtual |
| Difficult | Easy |
| Durable | Ephemeral |
| Profound | Superficial |
| Spiritual | Pragmatic |
| Costly | Inexpensive/free |
| Singular/Rare | Multiple/Numerous |
| Serene | Frantic |
| Complex | Simple |
| Coherent | Fragmented |
| Planned | Spontaneous |

[8] Writers often cite this statistic but do not consider the contexts, limitations and variants that are carefully delineated in the study. Jeffrey Smith and Lisa Smith, 'Spending Time with Art', *Empirical Studies of the Arts* 19 (2001), 229–36.

[9] Arden Reed, *Slow Art: The experience of looking, sacred images to James Turrell* (Oakland, CA: University of California Press, 2017), 12.

[10] Roberts, 'Slow Looking'.

[11] Jennifer Roberts, 'The Power of Patience: Teaching students the value of deceleration and immersive attention', *Harvard Magazine,* November–December 2013.

A notable exception is Shari Tishman's *Slow Looking: The art and practice of learning through observation* published in 2018. The textbook considers how slow looking might serve as a learning tool to help pupils investigate everything from doorknobs to radiation. Tishman explains how two aspects of her methodology may 'not fit with the larger trend' of slow looking. Specifically, Tishman explains that her approach to looking is 'not necessarily characterized by a quiet, meditative mood' nor is it 'anti-technology, even though the speed of digital life can pose a challenge to "slow"'.[12] It is worth noting, however, that when discussing art, Tishman describes quiet, systematic observation that falls in step with other discussions of slow looking.

## Beyond the White Cube: Fog and Flesh

Most of the exercises in slow looking that have featured in blogs and the popular press of the past decade focus predominantly on European and North American paintings made between the fifteenth and twentieth centuries. A small but growing number of artists and academics have applied the term 'slow art' to other genres such as site installations and film. In these discussions there is some slippage in applying the term to (1) art that takes a long time to make such as Robert Smithson's *Spiral Jetty*, (2) art that has a specific duration such as Andy Warhol's *Sleep* and (3) slow looking.[13] All of these meanings are used somewhat interchangeably in Arden Reed's, *Slow Art: The experience of looking, sacred images to James Turrell*, the only academic monograph to examine slow looking and art to date.[14] While some writers may point to the physical effort expended on the journey to the artwork or mention the use of a pencil and notebook, for the most part, the body is remarkably still and even wholly absent during the process of looking. Presumably, viewers might approach the painting to look more closely or from a slightly different perspective, but the role of motion and physicality is glossed over in the popular literature. The disembodied eye does all of the work while the other senses lie dormant. This approach is directly at odds

---

[12]  Tishman, *Slow Looking*, 4–5.

[13]  Grayson Perry, 'Slow Art It's the New Slow Food. No Really', *The Times*, 7 September 2005, https://www.thetimes.co.uk/article/slow-art-its-the-new-slow-food-no-really-cxl7lhx8zb5; 'Pursuit of Beauty: Slow Art,' *BBC Radio Seriously*, 8 June 2018, https://www.bbc.co.uk/programmes/p069dfql (both accessed 8 November 2018).

[14]  Arden, *Slow Art*.

with the frequent references to seeing 'in the flesh' and 'visceral' viewing in the literature on slow looking.[15] Possibly, the prominent role played by museums as initiators of or hosts to these exercises explains some of this restraint. While art institutions might enthusiastically embrace slow, meditative looking at a Jackson Pollock, they presumably would not wish for visitors to crawl over, under and around Duchamp's *Bicycle Wheel* or to lay on the floor for a different perspective on Michelangelo.

Even Reed's discussions of modern and contemporary works suggest a passive, contemplative engagement with the works. Visiting James Turrell's *Roden Crater* – an artwork that necessitates traveling to and through an extinct volcanic crater – Reed writes:

> Above me hung a circle of blue sky; at my feet a circle of black sand. Across from where I sat a disk of sunlight shot through the oculus. … I was watching time perform itself. I tried to grasp that what moved was not the patch of light but the support on which it shone, and along with the support, the room and myself and Arizona were all rotating together.[16]

Although the body is present and even acknowledged, the passive viewer sits in a sanitised and reflective state and space, watching and feeling the world go by. Reed suggests that the way *Roden Crater* 'leads you from one precisely staged and timed light show to another' recalls 'sacred medieval or secular Renaissance pageants'.[17] The allusion is revealing. Reed's conception of pre-modern pageants is more akin to works by Bill Viola than actual historical practice: a series of pauses, a *tableau vivant*. This sterilised conception of a pageant lacks the heaving multitudes, smells, noise and squirming bodies captured in the works of Pieter Bruegel the Elder or François Rabelais. Similarly, the carnage of blood, crushed flowers, tears and ambulances that follows in the wake of the penitent parades of the annual Filipino Passion performances are wholly absent. The medieval works cited by Reed are flat and timeless or at least portrayed that way. Referencing Hans Belting, Reed points to the plain gold backgrounds of icons, describing them as 'pictures, which seem to belong to a common space that allows one to meet the saints without respect to time or space'.[18]

---

[15]   For example, Roberts, 'Power of Patience' or Segler, 'Slow Knowing'.

[16]   Reed, *Slow Art*, 237.

[17]   Reed, *Slow Art*, 232. For images and descriptions of Roden Crater, see http://rodencrater.com/ (accessed 5 November 2018).

[18]   Reed, *Slow Art*, 68. In contrast, see Bissera Pencheva's *The Sensual Icon: Space, ritual, and the senses in Byzantium* (University Park, PA: Pennsylvania State University Press, 2010).

The viewing conditions invoked by the slow looking movement echo those described by Brian O'Doherty's *Inside the White Cube*:

> Art exists in a kind of eternity of display, and though there is lots of 'period' (late modern) there is no time. ... Indeed the presence of that odd piece of furniture, your own body, seems superfluous, an intrusion. The space offers the thought that while eyes and minds are welcome, space-occupying bodies are not.[19]

The intense focus of slow looking eradicates or rises above all distractions. We are not only shutting down our phones and laptops but also our bodies, other senses and other human beings. The references to serenity and mindfulness suggest that we are also quieting and dampening down emotions and certain aspects of ourselves. In our intense, singular focus upon the art object, we divorce it and ourselves from the rest of humanity, from the fluctuating and erratic pulse of a lived environment. Of most significant concern to art historical practice, this one-to-one, singular contemplation excludes all consideration of the object's original and subsequent audiences. There is only the object and myself. For three-dimensional and/or functional artworks and art historical analysis, this kind of static, singular gaze reduces the object to two dimensions.[20] One possible solution is that instead of slow, singular looking we instead consider the value of looking not once, but many times in all kinds of ways through a whole range of viewing platforms.

My first encounter with Clonmacnoise was far from the pristine scenarios found in the slow looking literature. Following a period of intense personal and professional upheaval, I did what many art historians do, surreptitiously wedging a quick site visit into a family holiday. Consequently, our time at Clonmacnoise was very short with just over an hour to view the original monuments inside the visitor centre and the concrete casts of the crosses in situ among the monastic buildings. The fog was so dense that the Shannon River had disappeared entirely even though it is located only a few metres from the crosses.[21] The plateau upon which the crosses and church stand seemed to float like an island in the mist. Alternately dragging and chasing a four-year-old, my viewing was fragmented but also

[19]    Brian O'Doherty, *Inside the White Cube: The ideology of the gallery space* (Santa Monica, CA: Lapis Press, 1986), 15.
[20]    See also, Catherine Karkov, this volume.
[21]    For images of Clonmacnoise in the fog, see https://bookbellandcross.com/ (accessed 12 November 2018).

visceral and physical. The rain was freezing, and we were all exhausted after a miserable night's sleep.

As art historians, we look in order to acquire knowledge, and I learned a few things in that brief hour. Although every colour photograph I had ever seen of the crosses of Clonmacnoise showed them resplendent on a green carpet of grass overlooking a blue river under sunny skies, it can be foggy and rainy in Ireland. The poor viewing conditions I experienced raised questions as to how weather transformed these crosses. A few months before my visit, Éamonn Ó Carragáin had given a conference paper suggesting that the iconographic programmes of the crosses unfolded 'sun-wise', but what about the effects of other weathers?[22] I also learned that four-year-olds endlessly delight in running in circles around crosses (both sun-wise and otherwise) rather than standing and methodically viewing all of the panels on the east side, then south, then west and north. This experience led me to thinking about how the iconographic programme might also be read laterally across registers rather than one face at a time. Essential to my current research project, the 60 cm difference between my height and that of my son instigated a consideration of scale and multiple, changing perspectives. Finally, my exhausted mental state prompted a reflection upon the role of emotion in the experience of artworks. Most of these 'discoveries' are obvious things. Of course, it rains in Ireland and the high crosses are very tall. Similarly, before visiting the high crosses, I had known that they would have been focal points during the Easter liturgy, but I had never considered the mental state of penitents emerging from forty days of fasting and – in some cases – isolation, near starvation and exile from the body of Christ, all capped off by one or more all-night vigils. Although the slow looking movement promotes discoveries of inherent features through lengthy perusal, the physical and uncontrolled nature of my viewing also suggested new avenues of research.

The common factor within all of my questions is the role of transformation – of weather, perspectives, mental and physical states, and pathways of viewing. Assessing these changes required looking slowly (over four seasons rather than the prescriptive three hours suggested by Roberts) but also repeatedly. Would

---

[22]   At a conference held at Princeton in March 2010, published as Éamonn Ó Carragáin, 'High Crosses, the Sun's Course, and Local Theologies at Kells and Monasterboice', in *Insular and Anglo-Saxon Art and Thought in the Early Medieval Period*, ed. Colum Hourihane (University Park, PA: Pennsylvania State University Press, 2011), 149–74. For a consideration of rainfall and monuments, see Heather Pulliam, 'Blood, Water and Stone: The performative cross', in *Making Histories: Proceedings of the Sixth International Conference in Insular Art*, ed. Jane Hawkes (Donington: Shaun Tyas, 2013), 262–78.

heavy rain 'animate' the cross in some way? How far would the shadow of the cross elongate in the setting sun of bright winter days? How would the presence of a few or many people affect the visual landscape that frames the crosses? In common with the slow looking movement, my approach is receptive but also embodied and multiple. It necessitates a consideration or envisioning of other viewpoints, including those that are not my own. All of this requires visiting and revisiting as well as visioning and revisioning.

## Casts, Prints and Digital Images:
### Supplementing the Fragmented Object

Medieval monuments do not survive in as good a condition as modern paintings. After a millennium of wind, ice and rain, the stone crosses are badly worn. Holes have permeated the high relief, and some figures have been reduced to little more than bulges in the stone. Clonmacnoise presents the spectator who wishes to view 'original works' with a dilemma. In the 1990s, the Office of Public Works moved the tenth-century sculptures into a purpose-built visitor centre. A cast of the Cross of the Scriptures now stands in place of the original. If these outdoor monuments are site-specific, their removal indoors makes it impossible to see the 'original' work as a coherent object. Even allowing for changes in landscape and the built environment, the removal indoors strips the sculpture of the light and effects of weather that animate and transform it into a performative piece. It is not that dissimilar to studying a film via stills rather than a moving image. Additionally, the fixed lighting embedded in the floor, while aiding legibility, works in direct opposition to natural light. Finally, the restricted space introduces strict limitations on viewing distances.

The fragmented, worn nature of the crosses inhibits the kind of singular viewing of the original advocated by the slow looking movement. Surrogate supplements are required. Peter Harbison's three-volume *The High Crosses of Ireland: An iconographical and photographic survey*, for example, translates the works into a medium that accommodates slow looking.[23] The fixed and regular perspective and distance of the reproductions allow a close, contemplative examination of the iconography of the crosses. Controlled lighting and black-and-white photography increase the legibility of worn features. The crosses are displayed like pinned bones in an antiquarian case allowing slow perusal and comparison. Measurements are given, but not scale. The crosses stand in a landscape devoid of people.

---

[23]    Peter Harbison, *The High Crosses of Ireland: An iconographical and photographic survey*, 3 vols (Bonn: Habelt, 1992).

In some instances, all of the background imagery has been cropped away so that the crosses float in the white void of the page.

The 3D ICONS project has created digital facsimiles of the crosses. The software makes it possible to consider different viewpoints and distances.[24] Like their print counterparts, these digital facsimiles give no real sense of scale or colour. Both print and digital facsimiles use artificially manipulated light. The latter does so in a way that cannot be duplicated in reality. Although rotational and zoomable, the object is isolated from human beings, animals, weather, sounds and the natural daylight that conveys the passing of time. At present, these scans have no obvious aesthetic value although undoubtedly that will change in a century or so, as has been the case with vinyl records and lantern slides. Plaster and concrete casts possess similar tactility, scale and structure as the original monuments. Crucially, in the case of the concrete casts at Clonmacnoise, their position outdoors also encompasses the surviving built and natural environment.

These facsimiles, in many ways, are far better facilitators of slow looking that the 'real' object. They fix the object, presenting it in a fashion that is accessible and uncluttered. Reproductions and plaster replicas allow slow reflection and long study unhampered by cold or rain. They do not, however, evoke the same aura as the original,[25] and they provide little or no reference to viewing environments and conditions. The concrete casts positioned outside prove the exception as they are animated by light and weather, framed by sweeping vistas, and contextualised by the topography, surviving graves and architectural features. Obviously, these are not the original surroundings – trees, buildings, walls, gravestones and corpses have changed a great deal[26] – but their presence reminds the viewer of integral aspects of the visual field that would otherwise be forgotten or neglected, especially the role of change and chance.

[24]    http://www.3dicons.ie/3d-content/sites/52-cross-scriptures-clonmacnoise #3d-model (accessed 1 November 2018).
[25]    Walter Benjamin, 'The Work of Art in the Age of Mechanical Reproduction', in *Illuminations*, ed. Hannah Arendt, trans. Harry Zohn (New York: Schocken Books, 1969), 221–4. For the topic of casts of medieval monuments and value, see Sally Foster and Sian Jones, 'The Untold Heritage Value and Significance of Replicas', *Conservation and Management of Archaeological Sites*, 21.1 (2019).
[26]    Bruno Latour and Adam Lowe have observed a similar phenomenon, recording audience responses to the installation of a facsimile of Veronese's *The Wedding at Cana* in its 'original' site, even though the building has undergone numerous changes and repairs. Bruno Latour and Adam Lowe, 'The Migration of the Aura or How to Explore the Original through Its Facsimiles', in *Switching Codes*, ed. Thomas Bartscherer and Roderick Coover (Chicago: University of Chicago Press, 2010), 275–97.

Jennifer Roberts states that for modern audiences three hours seems to be an unreasonable amount of time to ask viewers to contemplate a work of art.[27] Medieval monks at Clonmacnoise, however, lived with their crosses, a situation impossible for me to replicate. Many of the questions raised in my short visit to Clonmacnoise required specific weather conditions, and Irish weather is notoriously unpredictable. Short of moving to Clonmacnoise, my slow looking has had to stretch to multiple visits across at least a year, but even this is insufficient. After four trips, I have yet to experience the site in heavy rain, and there is no guarantee that my four days in December will deliver sufficient sunshine to check the length of shadows in winter. Again, facsimiles are necessary aids to my slow looking. The thousands of digital snapshots of Clonmacnoise available on the internet make it possible to investigate some of these questions. The very thing so frequently cited as the instigator for slow looking has, for me, become the means by which it can be achieved.

### Time, Weather and Bodies: Some Preliminary Findings

Time – historical, liturgical, and universal – is integral to the iconographic programmes of many Irish crosses, including that of the Cross of the Scriptures. Ó Carragáin has demonstrated that the programmes of many of the figurative crosses unfold throughout the day, following the movement of the sun. The presence of sundials on the Bewcastle Cross and a number of Irish crosses and cross-slabs make the connection between time, the sun and the crosses quite explicit.[28] Additionally, many of the figurative crosses begin with an image of Adam and Eve at the bottom of the cross, and Christ in Judgement dominating the cross-ring at the top, suggesting they encapsulate all of human history on a single monument. However, the crosses resist a linear, chronological approach to time. Like liturgy and exegesis, the panels do not follow a single narrative or historical arc but instead draw on many, possible paths across a network of connections.

---

[27]   Roberts, 'Slow Looking'.

[28]   Irish examples include one from Monasterboice, a monastic site that has two figurative crosses associated with the Cross of the Scriptures. Ann Hamlin, 'Some Northern Sundials and Time-Keeping in the Early Irish Church', in *Figures of the Past: Essays in Honour of A.M. Roe*, ed. E. Rynne (Dun Laoghaire: Glendale, 1987), 69–83; for a discussion of Bewcastle's sundial, see Fred Orton and Ian Wood with Clare A. Lees, *Fragments of History: Rethinking the Ruthwell and Bewcastle monuments* (Manchester: Manchester University Press, 2007), 131–43, and Catherine E. Karkov, *The Art of Anglo-Saxon England* (Woodbridge: Boydell, 2011), 68–79.

Among the many images on the Cross of the Scriptures at Clonmacnoise is the Hand of God, carved along the underside of the southern arm of the cross (Fig. 1).[29] The position is unusual in terms of Christian iconography, where the Hand is usually shown positioned above everything else. While affording the Hand prominence in scale, the artist has eschewed the more prominent and elevated faces of the Cross of the Scriptures as well the four panels of the capstone. Although the sun shines more on the south side than any other, the Hand remains in perpetual shadow throughout the course of the day in all seasons.

The Hand hangs suspended in the air like a question or command that awaits a human response and presence – whether real, imagined or remembered (Fig. 2). Emerging from the juncture between the cross and ring, the Hand simultaneously occupies several visual, physical and iconographic fields (Fig. 3). When viewing the east face of the cross from a short distance, the Hand hovers between the images of the cross-head and those on the shaft. As the former depicts the Last Judgement and the latter earthly events such as the *traditio clavium* and the foundation of Clonmacnoise, the Hand emerges from a seam between eschatological and historical time. Together, the images on the east side mark the establishment of at least three 'churches' – the eternal, heavenly church (Last Judgement), the church of Rome (*traditio clavium*) and that of Clonmacnoise.[30] The last of these is itself a conflation. The bottom panel depicts two figures, one tonsured and one in a short but ornate tunic with a sword, planting a post into the ground. The image closely resembles the establishment of Clonmacnoise as described in St. Ciarán's *vita* (Fig. 2). In the episode, Diarmait helps Ciarán raise the foundation stake. Many centuries later, a similar collaboration between abbot and king, in this instance Colman and Flann, created the Cross of the Scriptures and the stone church behind it.[31] Throughout the year, the rising sun strikes this panel before moving

[29] For colour images of the Cross of the Scriptures, see https://bookbelland-cross.com/ (accessed 12 November 2018).
[30] Also, as Maggie Williams notes, 'the juxtaposition of two depictions of the foundation and continuing prosperity of Clonmacnoise with an image of the ultimate source of Church authority links the history of the local community with the hub of Christianity'. Maggie Williams, 'The Sign of the Cross: Irish high crosses as cultural emblems', unpublished PhD dissertation, Columbia University, 2000, 132.
[31] See Harbison, *High Crosses* 1: 149, and Roger Stalley, 'Irish Sculpture of the Early Tenth Century and the Work of the "Muiredach Master": Problems of identification and meaning', *Proceedings of the Royal Irish Academy, Section C* 114 (2014), 141–79 at 157–63.

Fig. 1: South side of the Cross of the Scriptures (cast) in early evening light, showing Hand of God, two human heads and angel sheltering tonsured figure (photo: Stephenie McGucken)

Fig. 2: East side of the Cross of the Scriptures, showing Last Judgement, *traditio clavium* and the foundation of Clonmacnoise. The Hand of God is visible under the left arm of the cross (photo: Stephenie McGucken)

Fig. 3: Visitors at Clonmacnoise (photo: Stephenie McGucken).

up the shaft, further conveying a sense of cyclical beginnings and the continual renewal of God's church. Notably, the panel would be visible to audiences as they left the church, highlighting their role as part of this living and continuing chain. Marked graves were densely scattered in the ground surrounding the cross, and so the Hand of God blessed not only the church of the living but also that of the dead in a visceral and striking fashion.[32]

The Hand of God is omnipresent, visible from all perspectives – except from the north. The north had long been associated with sin and darkness. Figurative crosses, including the Cross of the Scriptures, frequently reserve the north for depictions of the devil and sinful creatures.[33] In an almost Miltonian sense of hell, the occluded Hand suggests the north with its deviant figures is a place without God. Those privileged to stand, kneel or walk directly under the Hand of God, however, might imagine themselves blessed and protected by God. On bright days, they too would be bathed in sunlight. Although beyond the reach of even the tallest member of the community, the scale of the Hand creates a sense of intimacy. Like the use of the first person in the language of the Psalms, the Hand's position creates a direct relationship between the individual and their God, a case of 'you', 'me' and 'us' rather than 'he', 'her' and 'they.'

The Hand of God as reproduced in Harbison's book does not fare well when compared to its glittering counterparts found in church mosaics or John's Gospel in the Codex Aureus of Charles the Bald. The latter is a psychedelic riot of colour and shape.[34] Executed in gold leaf and outlined in red against an azure diamond with bands of clouds circling in opposite directions, it conveys an incomprehensible, omnipotent divinity. Viewing the Clonmacnoise Hand of God in the 'flesh' (or concrete facsimile), however, is an entirely different matter. It is not possible to see the Hand of God when standing or kneeling directly under it without craning one's head back in an awkward fashion that is uncomfortable and disorienting.

---

[32] Although not discussing the Hand of God, the conception of the cross as unifying the community of the living and the dead buried beneath was first suggested by Williams, 'The Sign of the Cross', 124–44.

[33] Ó Carragáin, 'High Crosses', 153. For example, the Market Cross at Kells reserves the side that originally faced north for images of dismembered entangled figures and a horned and tailed figure supported by beasts.

[34] Bayerische Staatsbibliothek ms. Clm. 14000, fol. 97v, digitised manuscript available via Digitale-sammlungen.de (accessed 5 November 2018).

On sunny, windy days – which Ireland possesses in abundance –
clouds race across the blue sky creating bursts of shadow and light, further
heightening the sense of dizzying motion. The cognitive effects are not
that different from those created by the whirling shapes and colour that
decorate continental images of the Hand of God, nor even of the glittering tesserae surrounding Mediterranean ones – except in Ireland, the
heavens do move. From sunrise to early afternoon on sunny days, the arm
of the cross casts a partial shadow on the panel beneath, which depicts
an angel whose outspread wings shelter a tonsured figure (Fig. 1).[35] The
shadow's effects might recall Exodus 33:22, when God tells Moses, 'And
when my glory will cross over, I will set you in a cleft of the rock, and
I will protect you with my right hand, until I pass by.' On rainy days,
the sculpture's transformation can be even more spectacular. The arm
provides some shelter, but not much. It is sufficient, however, to create a
small column of stillness between the viewer's eye and the Hand of God.
The drops of rain collect and fall from the arm's edges at a slightly slower
rate than those that race from the sky to the ground. The effect is of time
moving around the spectator at different speeds while they stay perfectly
still, centred by the Hand of God.

## Completing the Circuit: The Embodied Eye

Academic illustrations of Clonmacnoise typically occlude human presence; and yet, slow looking at Clonmacnoise inevitably involves nego-
tiating the ebb and flow of busloads of visitors who arrive and depart
throughout the day. On 9 September each year, pilgrims and the clergy
join the usual crowds of tourists to mark St. Ciarán's Feast Day. The day
involves a Mass and responsory prayers at various sites. In 2018, both the
wind and the short but steep climb up the plateau proved challenging to
the aging congregation, many of whom needed support and assistance
while walking.

These crowds are salient reminders that human beings are not impedi-
ments to viewing the crosses but rather an integral part of their function and frame. The crosiers held by the figures carved onto the cross
echoed those held by living abbots and priests. While most of the liturgy
at medieval Clonmacnoise undoubtedly took place indoors, essential
rituals such as the lighting of the Maundy Thursday candle most likely
occurred at the church door in front of which stood the Cross of the

---

[35]   The photograph used in this essay was taken in the early evening in order to
maximise legibility.

Scriptures. The anthropomorphic gesture of hugging a cross (or its cast) practised by one or two bolder and younger pilgrims and the faltering steps of the older ones are useful reminders that Insular monks formed crosses with their bodies when they prayed, often in penance, in what was known then as the *crossfigell* pose and today might be termed a 'stress position'.[36] When a small group stands before the east side of the Cross of the Scriptures, the inverted dove in the medallion beneath Christ's feet appears to descend upon them, evoking depictions of Pentecost and the sense of divine benediction.

More intimately, when kneeling before the east face of the Cross of the Scriptures, the three somewhat anomalous crosses that decorate Christ's body in its death shroud might easily be touched or kissed. The Durrow Cross, which may have been made by the same artist, has a similarly positioned panel depicting a large tonsured figure flanked by angels.[37] Two seated tonsured figures hold a book open before him. When kneeling before the cross, the two seated figures appear to look at the book while twisting in three-quarter profiles so that their combined gaze includes 'you'. The five figures create a circle that becomes complete through the presence of an audience. From this perspective, it is clear that the book is held open as much to the kneeling viewer as to those depicted in the panel. The position and prominence of the open book also seem to invite kissing or touching.

Undoubtedly, all artworks might benefit from slow looking and study. The fragmented, worn and three-dimensional nature of many early medieval works requires it, but also necessitates multiple viewings, through many, varied platforms – including those that might be seen as the antithesis of slow viewing. It may be the serendipitous, digital photo taken during a thirty-minute whirlwind bus tour that captures the falling raindrop or long shadow in a moment of sunlight. Borrowing from phenomenology, we might supplement the emphasis upon stillness and the transcendental with an equal consideration of visceral embodied viewing and viewers. Similarly, we might look with an 'ecological eye' that recognises that 'art history needs to widen the objects of its obsessions, beyond visual culture and media, outwards towards the human and other-than-

---

[36] Carol A. Farr, *The Book of Kells: Its function and audience* (London: British Library, 1997), 106–8.
[37] For image, see https://bellbookandcross.com/ (accessed 12 November 2018). For discussion of the artist and connections between the two crosses, see Stalley, 'Irish Sculpture'.

human vectors that animate the planet and its ecosystems'.[38] In so doing, we recognise that art, especially those monuments created, animated and shaped by and in the natural world, does not exist solely in the vacuum of the white cube or page.

[38]   Andrew Patrizio, *The Ecological Eye: Assembling an ecocritical art history* (Manchester: Manchester University Press, 2018), 3.

# Thinking about Stone:
# An Elemental Encounter with the Ruthwell Cross

## CATHERINE E. KARKOV

> *We are tired of McDonald's hamburgers.*
> *We want something slow cooked.*[1]

2014 was, at least for art historians, the year in which interest in the slow began to appear everywhere. There were several articles, including a much-cited one in *Harvard Magazine*,[2] multiple blogs and a lot of discussion in various e-fora. Slow lesson plans and exercises were shared and their merits debated on the Material Collective's Facebook page. These were followed rapidly and inevitably by calls for examples of the merits of fast learning and various posts about exercises involving the use of Twitter in the classroom, and so forth. There was a certain amount of rejection of, or at least reaction against, the all-pervasive digital and its culture of remedia-tion, text and immediate access, and a corresponding renewal of interest in a return to the digits and the work of the hand and fingers, an interest that was clearly part of a much larger concern to reclaim the craft exer-cised by the human body, and the focus of the unplugged mind.[3] Several of the exercises posted to the Material Collective, for example, involved 'slow looking', asking students to sit in front of a work of art, all electronic devices turned off, for what was deemed to feel to them like an unreason-ably lengthy amount of time and to just look, slowly and carefully, and to write – with pen or pencil – about what was seen, and/or to draw the work of art.[4] (There is no better way to get to know a work of art than

---

[1]    Lindsay Waters, *Enemies of Promise: Publishing, perishing, and the eclipse of scholarship* (Chicago: University of Chicago Press, 2004), 82.

[2]    Jennifer L. Roberts, 'The Power of Patience: Teaching students the value of deceleration and immersive attention', *Harvard Magazine*, November–December 2013, harvardmagazine.com/2013/11the-power-of-patience (accessed 23 November 2018).

[3]    See for example, Robert Sennett, *The Craftsman* (Harmondsworth: Penguin, 2009); Nicholas Carr, *The Shallows: How the Internet is changing the way we think, read and remember* (London: Atlantic Books, 2010).

[4]    A number of studies have appeared since that document the ways in which the use of the hand – handwritten class notes, for example – focuses the mind and

to try and recreate it with your own hands.) Slow looking exercises were designed to make students think deeply about what they were looking at, how it was made and how it made meaning through its physical presence and materials, but it also got them back to the object and away from the mediated or remediated image – although all art, even that encountered personally, is, of course, mediated. What was not mentioned anywhere in the posts, at least as far as I have been able to discover, was that sitting in front of a work of art, looking, writing, drawing, watching it change as the light changes, takes us back to the origins of art history as a discipline. This is precisely how generations of early scholars and students learned and wrote about art. Johan Winckelmann and Gotthold Lessing's publications on the Laocoön (and other classical sculptures) are arguably the best-known examples of this type of work,[5] but the importance of this method of encountering art surfaces more recently in, for example, T.J. Clark's book *The Sight of Death, an Experiment in Art Writing*.[6] For this book, Clark spent six months at the Getty, returning every morning to record his responses to the same two Poussin paintings that were hung together in one room: *Landscape with a Man Killed by a Snake* (1648) and *Landscape with Calm* (1650–1). As with the cooking and eating of slow food, such exercises in slow scholarship not only take us back to the profession's practical origins, they also invite and express prolonged enjoyment, something increasingly difficult to experience in the modern, neoliberal, metric-obsessed university.

Until the time came for *Landscape with a Man Killed by a Snake* to be returned to the National Gallery in London, the two paintings Clark wrote about were not visibly going anywhere, and his title referred in the first instance to death as a subject of the works he was studying. They are also works carefully conserved and preserved within atmospherically controlled environments and tended lovingly by museum conservators. Most of the surviving corpus of Anglo-Saxon stone sculpture, on the other hand, is still in situ or housed in far less protected environments.

---

improves the retention of ideas compared to the use of computers, tablets and so forth. See, for example, http://www.theatlantic.com/technology/archive/2014/05/to-remember-a-lecture-better-take-notes-by-hand/361478/ (accessed 23 November 2018).

[5]    Johan J. Winckelmann, *Geschichte der Kunst des Alterthums* (Dresden, 1764); Gotthold E. Lessing, *Laokoön oder Über die Grenzen der Malerei und Poesie mit beiläufigen Erläuterungen verschiedener Punkte der alten Kunstgeschichte* (Berlin, 1766).

[6]    T.J. Clark, *The Sight of Death, an Experiment in Art Writing* (New Haven, CT: Yale University Press, 2006).

It is going somewhere. It is slowly eroding and decaying as experienced in human time, or doing so rather more rapidly, as experienced in the geological time that embraces the life cycle of stone. This is slow sculpture, full of breaks, fractures, wear, the traces of centuries of use, abuse and conflicts. To really understand it as sculpture, as art that exists through changing time and place, the way Clark understood Poussin's paintings, we have to return to it again and again, not over a matter of months, but over years, decades, even centuries. And in the end, all we can really know is the monument as it exists in our own lifetime. One sculpture, then, can become a life's work, work not in the sense of understanding what it means, but in the sense of understanding what it *is*. This is not a mode of research and scholarship universities now want. It is not work that can be produced and published quickly. It has little if any 'impact', that all-important research element in the corporate university. It can be repetitious, can produce notes rather than articles and monographs. It also cannot be captured through digital modelling, in fact it cannot be captured at all. No picture or text will ever capture the experience of this type of slow scholarship as it relies on being there in the sculpture's presence, its place and environment; picture and text can only describe or capture moments of that experience.

This essay presents a long slow think about the eighth-century Ruthwell Cross (Dumfries), a monument to which numerous scholars have returned again and again over the centuries, one to which some academic careers have been all but devoted, and one to which I have returned myself time and again for nearly thirty years. We can attempt to capture the Ruthwell monument digitally – indeed, I am part of a team that has attempted to do just that.[7] We might be able to recover some of its badly damaged inscriptions and some of the details of its carvings. We can recreate and animate its creators, speed up its inevitable decay, add colour, model its original landscape setting, and so forth. Yet despite our best efforts, all the attention it has received, the centuries of people looking at it, discussing, debating, drawing, photographing and arguing over the cross, it still eludes us. Meaning is carved into it. Meaning emerges from it. Meaning circles around it, elusive and just out of our grasp. I've written about the first two sorts of meaning repeatedly, but now I want to find the time to write about the latter. I want to think about those meanings that circle the cross, that spiral backwards and forwards through history, that haunt the

---

[7]    With Daniel Paul O'Donnell, Wendy Osborn and Roberto Rosselli Del Turco, 'The Visionary Cross: An experiment in the multimedia edition', *Digital Humanities* (2007), 143–5.

cross and its history, and that can't always be pinned down within historical sources. The cross is elemental, the creation of earth, fire, water and
air. I want to think about what that means to the meaning of the cross.

The Ruthwell monument is itself slow. As Jane Bennett observes of
things in general, their

> rate of speed and … pace of change are *slow* compared to the duration
> and velocity of the human bodies participating in and perceiving them.
> 'Objects' appear as such because their *becoming* proceeds at a speed or
> a level below the threshold of human discernment.[8]

The Ruthwell Cross came into being slowly. It took time to design and
carve, and the best way to understand how it was designed is, as so many
art historians seem now to be rediscovering, to spend a lot of time slow
looking, coming slowly to discover all its details, and how these details
(and hence the messages conveyed by the cross) change in changing
light, with the seasons and in different weather. This is how the Anglo-
Saxons would have experienced the cross, and while I am not claiming or
attempting to recreate their experience, I am attempting to experience the
cross in and as place and environment, in slow time, so as an experience
of time and place something like what they might have known. This is
a form of scholarship, and a form of removing oneself from the confines
of the university in order to practise scholarship that is being taken up
increasingly by medievalist art historians worldwide.[9]

## Earth

To begin at the beginning. The Ruthwell Cross was originally carved
from two pieces of sandstone, possibly from the same quarry. According
to the Geological Survey Report on the monument written in 2004, the
massive lower stone is a pale pinkish-grey medium-grained quartz-rich
sandstone, non-micacious, and with a low percentage of feldspar. The
fragments of the smaller upper stone are pale red quartz-rich medium- to
coarse-grained sandstone, the grains coated in iron oxide and less uniform
in size than those of the lower stone. Both are thought to have been quar-
ried from the same bed (or beds) of Carboniferous mixed sandstone and

---

[8]   Jane Bennett, *Vibrant Matter: A political ecology of things* (Durham, NC:
Duke University Press, 2010), 58.
[9]   See, for example, the Migrating Art Historians project: https://www.indiegogo.
com/projects/migrating-art-historians-innovative#/ (accessed 23 November 2018).

Fig. 1: The Ruthwell Cross

limestone that underlies the area.[10] The stone has life. It has its origins in water and the centuries-long processes of sand and marine sedimentation it deposits. The cross emerged from the ground of this area. It is place, and it is in place – though not its original one. Originally it would have stood out-of-doors, rising up from the earth. Today, set in a pit in a specially built apse inside the church at Ruthwell, it looks trapped (Fig. 1). Did it need to be confined? Was someone afraid it might fly away?

Isidore of Seville wrote of stone that it had the ability to capture and imitate the sound of the human voice. This type of stone he called *icon*, although his source, Pliny, called it *echo*. More specifically, he wrote, 'It is *icon* in Greek and "image" (*imago*) in Latin, because an image of someone else's speech is produced in response to one's voice.'[11] Icon, echo and image: certainly the Anglo-Saxons must have understood the stone of the Ruthwell Cross in this way as it is all three things, and all three things emerge from it. Icon as *imago*, especially as religious image imported from Rome, and echo as the traces of the human voice that remain in the runic poem on the crucifixion inscribed in the borders of the cross's two narrow sides, are two of the features for which the cross is most frequently studied. Together image and voice present us with a complex liturgical programme narrated through figural icons and meditative verse,[12] as well as a powerful political statement about the expansion and authority of the Northumbrian church and kingdom, an authority centred in both Northumbrian Englishness and Roman spirituality.[13] But the cross's icons and echoes are images and voices from elsewhere and from different times. Its icons of Christ, Mary and the saints translate a spiritual community to this place to become part of the Ruthwell community. Its echoes include the voice of the True Cross of the crucifixion. It is not *just* stone; it is also wood growing (originally) up from the earth, surrounded by trees and birds, sun and water.

The cross is both stone and wood always, the one continually evident within and through the other like the blood and gold of the cross in *The*

[10]   Andrew A. McMillan, 'Examination of Stone I the Ruthwell Monument, 3. Observations from Site Visit, 19 August, 2004', British Geological Survey, Edinburgh, Report EE04/0651.

[11]   Isidore of Seville, *The Etymologies of Isidore of Seville*, ed. Stephen A. Barney et al. (Cambridge: Cambridge University Press, 2006), 319.

[12]   See especially, Éamonn Ó Carragáin, *Ritual and the Rood: Liturgical images and the Old English poems of the Dream of the Rood tradition* (London & Toronto: Toronto University Press, 2005).

[13]   See especially, Fred Orton and Ian Wood, with Clare A. Lees, *Fragments of History: Rethinking the Ruthwell and Bewcastle monuments* (Manchester: Manchester University Press, 2007).

*Dream of the Rood*, which echoes the Ruthwell poem. Paulinus of Nola (354–431) wrote that

> Indeed the Cross of inanimate wood has living power, and since its discovery it has lent its wood to countless, almost daily prayers of men. Yet it suffers no diminution; though daily divided, it seems to remain whole to those who lift it, and always entire to those who venerate it. Assuredly it draws this power of incorruptibility, this undiminishing integrity, from the Blood of that Flesh which endured death yet did not see corruption.[14]

Perhaps the cross originally held a relic of the True Cross, wood enclosed in stone. I wonder if the Anglo-Saxons would have agreed with Paulinus that the wood of the True Cross was inanimate as such a variety of objects, many of them wooden, are given the ability to speak in the material record, as well as in the Old English Riddles, to which I will return. The woodenness (or treeness) of the Ruthwell Cross is an essential feature of the monument, and one conjured by the stone itself. Treeness, or woodenness, is also a well-known feature of the cross in *The Dream of the Rood*, which is adamantly (though not exclusively) *treow* or *wudu* throughout the poem: the best of trees (*syllicre treow*), the saviour's tree (*hælendes treow*), the gallows-tree (*gealg-treow*), the best of wood (*wudu selest*), and so forth.[15] It also narrates its own transformation from tree to cross, making clear its existence as two distinct, yet identical, living things in the landscape:

> Þæt wæs geara iu        ic þæt gyta geman
> þæt ic wæs aheawen        holtes on ende,
> astyred of stefne minum.        Genaman me ðær strange feondas,
> geworhton him þær to wæfer-syne        heton me heora wergas hebban.

'It was long ago, I remember it still, that I was cut down at the edge of the wood, removed from my roots. Strange enemies seized me there, made me into a spectacle, commanded me to raise up their criminals'. (lines 28–31)[16]

---

[14]   Paulinus of Nola, *Letters of St. Paulinus of Nola*, trans. P.G. Walsh, 2 vols (Westminster: Paulist Press, 1967), letter 31.6, pp. 132–3.

[15]   On the terminology for the cross in the poem, see Andy Orchard, 'The Dream of the Rood: Cross-references', in *New Readings in the Vercelli Book*, ed. Samantha Zacher and Andy Orchard (Toronto: University of Toronto Press, 2009), 225–53.

[16]   Mary Clayton, ed. and trans., *Old English Poems of Christ and His Saints* (Cambridge, MA: Harvard University Press, 2013), 162.

The Ruthwell Cross does not need to tell its biography in this way because it shows us this transformation visually. The inhabited vine-scrolls around which the runic poem is inscribed figure the cross as a tree filled with animals that feed on its fruit as they would on those of a living tree in the woods (Figs 2 and 3). The vine-scrolls fill the panels in which they are carved, while the twig-like runes extend their being as tree out into the borders that surround them. Stone becomes wood and speaks as such. In its original position these vine-scrolls would have appeared to grow upwards from roots buried deep in the ground – in fact the base of the vine appearing to emerge from the ground is one of the most striking aspects of the vine-scrolls at both Ruthwell (Fig. 4) and the cross at Bewcastle with which it is so often linked. And in its original position the cross would have stood like a tree in the landscape, expressing its own essential woodenness.

It was certainly believed to have the ability to grow like a tree in modern times. William Nicolson, bishop of Carlisle, and a student and teacher of Old English at Oxford, visited the cross in April 1697 and again in July 1704. He was impressed by its great height, even though at this point it was lying in pieces on the floor of the church, some of its fragments buried beneath the earth from which they had come. While there, he recorded a local story that apparently remained current in various tellings and retellings throughout the eighteenth century:

The common Tradition of yᵉ Original of this stone is this: It was found, letter'd and entire, in a Stone-Quarry on the Shore (a good way within yᵉ Sea-mark) call'd Rough-Scarr. Here it had lain long admir'd, when (in a Dream) a neighbouring Labourer was directed to yoke four Heifers of a certain Widow y liv'd near him; and when they stop'd with yⁱʳ Burthen, there to slack his Team, erect yᵉ Cross & build a Church over it: All which was done accordingly. I wonder'd to see a Company of Modern Presbyterians (as yᵉ present parishoners profess yᵐselves to be) so steady in this Faith; and even to believe, yet further, yᵗ the Cross was not altogether so long (at its first erection) as was afterwards: But that it miraculously grew, like a Tree, till it touched the Roof of the Church.[17]

[17]    William Nicolson, 'Bishop Nicolson's Diaries: Part II', ed. H. Ware, *Transactions of the Cumberland and Westmorland Antiquarian and Archaeological Society*, new series 2 (1902), 155–230, at 196.

Fig. 2: The Ruthwell Cross, inhabited vine-scroll, original north side

Fig. 3: The Ruthwell Cross, inhabited vine-scroll, original south side

Fig. 4: The Ruthwell Cross, base of inhabited vine-scroll

## Fire

Isidore of Seville also wrote of limestone that it

> is said to be alive, because even when it has become cold to the touch it
> still retains some fire concealed inside, so that when water is poured on
> it the hidden fire bursts forth. It has this marvellous characteristic: once
> it has been set on fire, it burns in water, which usually extinguishes fire,
> and it is extinguished in oil, which usually kindles fire.[18]

Sandstone is not limestone, but the beds that underlie the area are of
mixed sandstone and limestone, and I wonder if the Anglo-Saxons would
have distinguished between the two anyway. The upper stone is red, and
the lower one a pinkish-grey. Heather Pulliam has written of the latter that
its pink 'seems to pulse within the grey'.[19] Little pinkish glowing embers. It
burns with a life force. This effect would have been even more pronounced
when the cross stood out-of-doors, lit by sunlight. It might, of course,
also have been heightened when the stone was glistening with rain. In
the Christian tradition, Christ was associated with fire,[20] and the Anglo-
Saxons might have understood the cross as burning with spiritual life and
the Passion of Christ. Fire sparked in the unborn John the Baptist's recognition of Christ at the Visitation, it was in Mary's womb at the Annunciation,
it flamed in the lamb of God and in the inspiration under which the four
evangelists wrote their gospels. The fire held within the limestone, Isidore
tells us, only burned more brightly within the stone when it was covered
with water. This may well have happened when rain coated the stone,
perhaps making some of its figures appear to weep,[21] and bringing to life
the sacraments of baptism and the eucharist symbolised by the figural panels
on the monument's original eastern and western faces respectively.[22]

---

[18]   Isidore of Seville, *The Etymologies of Isidore of Seville*, 319.
[19]   Heather Pulliam, 'Blood, Water and Stone: The performative cross', in
*Making Histories: Proceedings of the 6th International Conference on Insular Art,
York 2011*, ed. Jane Hawkes (Donington: Shaun Tyas, 2013), 262–78, at 267.
[20]   See further Carol Neuman de Vegvar, 'The Echternach Lion: A leap of faith',
in *The Insular Tradition*, ed. Catherine E. Karkov, Michael Ryan and Robert T.
Farrell (Albany, NY: SUNY Press, 1997), 167–88, at 175–6.
[21]   Pulliam, 'Blood, Water and Stone: The performative cross'.
[22]   The original orientation of the monument is hypothesised based on comparison with that of the Bewcastle Cross, which is still in situ, and the west
face of which has two scenes in common with Ruthwell. For the history of the
monument's destruction and reconstruction, see below.

## Water

At the crucifixion blood and water, the two liquids of the sacraments, poured from the wound in Christ's side. The Ruthwell Cross tells us in its runic poem that 'ic miþ blodæ bistemid, bigoten...' ('I was drenched with blood begotten...' – presumably from Christ's side, at least that is what the echo of these lines in the later poem *The Dream of the Rood* tells us). Indeed, it is this blood that the Anglo-Saxons would have understood as giving the cross its life, its voice, its power of performance. As Paulinus of Nola made clear, it was the blood absorbed into the True Cross at the crucifixion that caused the wood to partake of Christ's substance, giving it the power of regeneration so that its fragments were never diminished,[23] as well as giving it the ability to reproduce itself in multiple forms. Relics of the True Cross had the power to turn wood – other fragments of wood, the wood of the reliquaries that contained them – into further relics of the Cross.[24] Perhaps Ruthwell did hold a relic, perhaps a relic of the True Cross, but it is not necessary for it to have done so in order for it to perform as the True Cross. It is speaking. It is speaking through the twig-like runes of the poem. The blood it speaks of flows down over its inhabited vine-scrolls (Figs 2 and 3), nourishing them as they rise upward from the earth, their branches filled with ripe berry bunches symbolic of that very blood. In its original position the vines would have appeared to have roots growing deep into the soil (Fig. 4). The blood flows down over the faithful, the community depicted on the cross, the community that would at times have been washed with rain, some appearing to weep.

The Ruthwell Cross was also the product of water, the sea that once flowed over the area, depositing its layers of sediment. It had a watery birth. By the nineteenth century its birth by water had been reimagined and retold in a story that had it miraculously washed ashore from a shipwreck. 'The pillar is said to have been brought by sea from some distant country, and to have been cast on shore by shipwreck.' The Reverend Henry Duncan, who recorded this legend, didn't give it much credence, but he did note that there may have been some element of truth behind it:

---

[23] See above, note 14.

[24] On this aspect of relics of the True Cross, see S.T.R.O. d'Ardenne, 'The Old English Inscriptions on the Brussels Cross', *English Studies* 21:16 (1939), 145–64 at 145–6; Anne Van Ypersele de Strihou, *Le Trésor de la Cathedrale des Saints Michel et Gudule à Brussels* (Brussels: np, 2000), 35.

It is not improbable that this tradition may bear some vague reference to the period when the alteration took place in the form, and perhaps also in the object, of the column, at which time its site may possibly have been changed. It is remarkable that the remains of an ancient road, founded on piles of wood leading through a morass to the Priestside (which is a stripe of arable land enclosed between this morass and the shore of the Solway Firth), were in existence in the last thirty or forty years.[25]

Did the cross once stand near the shore – many have suggested so – its bleeding and weeping stone looking out over the water? Was it once a beacon to travellers, exiles, those in danger of shipwreck?

### Air

Arrows fly by air, birds fly through the air. I've long been fascinated by the little image of the archer firing an arrow carved into the lowest arm of the cross-head on the original east face of the cross (Fig. 5). He is so often overlooked – indeed, it took years for me to really notice him and longer still for him to fully capture my attention. He's a puzzle. He doesn't quite seem to fit in with the baptismal significance of all the panels carved beneath him. He is also shown in dynamic motion, while the rest of the figures stand relatively still. But I have come, over the years, to regard him as a key part of Ruthwell's meaning. At what is he firing? At what is he not firing? He was probably intended to be firing his arrow at the eagle (a symbol of Christ) perched on a branch that originally capped this side of the cross-head (Fig. 6). He may be firing at the cross itself. Perhaps he is firing at both. Generations of scholars have looked to the Bible, patristics, the liturgy and commentary on it for an answer. Ernst Kantorowicz and Della Hooke have identified him as Ismael.[26] Meyer Schapiro believed he was a hunter with apotropaic significance.[27] Fritz Saxl and Bob Farrell

---

[25]   Henry Duncan, 'An Account of the Remarkable Monument in the Shape of a Cross, inscribed with Roman and Runic Letters, preserved in the Garden of Ruthwell Manse, Dumfriesshire', *Archaeologia Scotica* IV part 2 (1833), 313–26, at 317. Duncan's paper includes an interpretation of the runic inscriptions by Thorleifur Gudmundson that is grossly inaccurate.

[26]   Ernst Kantorowicz, 'The Archer on the Ruthwell Cross', *Art Bulletin* 42.1 (1960), 57–9.

[27]   Meyer Schapiro, 'The Bowman and the Bird on the Ruthwell Cross and Other Works: The interpretation of secular themes in early medieval religious art', *Art Bulletin* 45 (1963), 351–5; Della Hooke, 'Christianity and the "Sacred Tree"', in M.D.J. Bintley and M.G. Shapland, eds, *Trees and Timber in the Anglo-Saxon World* (Oxford: Oxford University Press, 2013), 228–50, at 239.

Fig. 5: The Ruthwell Cross, archer

Fig. 6: The Ruthwell Cross, eagle on branch

believed him to be the devil firing arrows of heresy and ignorance.[28] Éamonn Ó Carragáin, developing an idea first put forward by Barbara Raw,[29] has argued that the panel should be read through the writings of Gregory the Great and Bede, specifically Gregory the Great's *Moralia in Job*, Book xix, chapter 30, in which Gregory expands on the two natures of the bow: 'in sacred writings under the name of the bow are signified, at times, the attacks of the wicked; at times, the day of judgement; and at times indeed the sacred writings themselves'.[30] In his commentary on verse 9 of the Canticle of Habakkuk, Bede took Gregory's statement to refer

> to those who teach God's revelation, through whom 'you [Christ] will give warning of your Judgement which is suddenly to come, so that whoever will be terrified by the warning of your anger as though at a drawn bow, and takes care to beg your mercy, will not feel the arrow-shot that is the warning of eternal punishments'.[31]

Perhaps some did read all this into the image, but it is really not necessary to look beyond the monument for an explanation of the panel. The cross expresses itself quite clearly through its own materials, images and words. The cross says '[ic] miþ strelum giwundad' ('[I] was wounded by arrows'), a line echoed in *The Dream of the Rood*:

---

[28] Fritz Saxl, 'The Ruthwell Cross', *Journal of the Warburg and Courtauld Institutes* 6 (1943), 1–19, at 6; Robert T. Farrell, 'The Archer and Associated Figures on the Ruthwell Cross – A reconsideration', in *Bede and Anglo-Saxon England: Papers in honour of the 1300th anniversary of the birth of Bede, given at Cornell University in 1973 and 1974*, ed. Robert T. Farrell, British Archaeological Reports, British Series 46 (Oxford: British Archaeological Reports, 1978), 96–117.

[29] Barbara Raw, 'The Archer, the Eagle and the Lamb', *Journal of the Warburg and Courtauld Institutes* 30 (1967), 391–4.

[30] Ó Carragáin, *Ritual and the Rood*, 141, citing Gregory the Great, *Gregorius Magnus, Moralia in Iob*, ed. Marcus Adriaen, CCSL 143A, 143B (Turnhout: Brepols, 1979–85), 998–1002, at 999: 'arcus autem nomine in sacro eloquio aliquando malorum insidiae, aliquando dies iudicii, aliquando uero ipsa eadem sacra eloquia designantur'.

[31] Ó Carragáin, *Ritual and the Rood*, 141, trans. Bede, *In Habacuc*, ed. J.E. Hudson, CCSL 119B (Turnhout: Brepols, 1983), 394; Seán Connolly, trans., *On Tobit and the Canticle of Habkkuk* (Dublin: Four Courts Press, 1997), 79.

> Forleton me þa hilderincas
> standan steame bedrifenne;      eall ic wæs mid strælum forwundod.[32]

'The warriors left me standing drenched in blood; I was all wounded by arrows' (lines 61b–62).

And here is the archer firing his arrows (Fig. 5). The archer and the eagle can then be understood as a straightforward symbolic crucifixion as narrated by the cross on which they appear.

Arrows are an unusual, if not unique, feature of the crucifixion at Ruthwell and in *The Dream of the Rood*, at least at this early date in European art. While it is possible that the meaning of *stræl* (arrow) might extend to include a pointed object more generally, according to the former director of the Toronto *Dictionary of Old English* it appears to be used exclusively to refer to an arrow or dart,[33] with *strælian* meaning to shoot an arrow and *strælbora* being an archer. The noun (*strelum*) in the inscription is in the plural, so it cannot refer to the spear that according to convention made the wound in Christ's side. The Ruthwell archer may then be the origin for this particular representation of the crucifixion in Anglo-Saxon England. It is the archer's arrows that let flow the streams of blood and water that give voice to the cross and give birth to the community of believers depicted on the shaft of the cross, as well as the community of believers who had the cross made.

The bow is as important as the arrows. The bow had a life-cycle very like that of the cross, and it was a *pliable* living weapon. Exeter Book Riddle 73, the answer to which has now been accepted as 'bow',[34] begins with the lines

> Ic on wonge aweox,      wunode þær mec feddon
> hruse ond heofonwolcn,      oþþæt me onhwyrfdon
> gearum frodne,      þa me grome wurdon,
> of þære gecynde      þe ic ær cwic beheold,
> onwendon mine wisan,      wegedon mec of earde,

---

[32]   Clayton, ed., *Old English Poems of Christ and His Saints*, 164. All translations of the Old English are my own unless otherwise stated.

[33]   Pers. comm., Antonette diPaolo Healey.

[34]   A.N. Doane, 'Three Old English Implement Riddles: Reconsiderations of numbers 4, 49, and 73', *Modern Philology* 84 (1987), 243–57, at 254–6; Jennifer Neville, 'The *Exeter Book Riddles*' Precarious Insights into Wooden Artefacts', in *Trees and Timber in the Anglo-Saxon World*, ed. Bintley and Shapland, 122–43, at 131.

gedydon þæt ic sceolde          wiþ gesceape minum
on bonan willan          bugan hwilum          (lines 1–7)[35]

('I grew in a field, dwelt where the earth and the clouds of heaven fed
me, until men who were hostile to me turned me, old in years, away
from the nature I held while alive. They changed my condition, carried
me out of my homeland, made it so that sometimes against my nature
I had to bow to the will of a killer.')

Riddle 53, the answer to which *may* be bow, or cross, or gallows tree,
or flail,[36] begins similarly

Ic seah on bearwe          beam hlifian,
tanum torhtne.          Þæt treow wæs on wynne,
wudu weaxende.          Wæter hine ond eorþe
feddan fægre,          oþþæt he frod dagum
on oþrum wearð          aglachade
deope gedolgod,          dumb in bendum,
wriþen ofer wunda,          wonnum hyrstum
foran gefrætwed. (lines 1–8a)[37]

('I saw in a grove a towering tree bright in its branches. That tree was
joyful, the growing wood. Water and earth fed it beautifully, until,
old in days, it was turned into a different state, one of misery, deeply
wounded, voiceless in bonds, its wounds tied over, adorned with dark
ornaments in front.')

Both poems echo the words of the cross in *The Dream of the Rood*,
words that, as I argued above, the Ruthwell Cross does not need to speak
as it shows us the growing process in its vine-scroll, and speaks it to us
as cut and wounded instrument of death in its runic poem. The arrows
from the bow that wound the cross even further help to strengthen that
connection. The movement from tree to weapon and the essential living-
ness of these things persist. Both cross and bow began life as trees growing
undisturbed in woods or field, up from the ground into the air, until
enemies cut them down and refashioned them. Both endured an inner

---

[35]    Bernard J. Muir, *The Exeter Anthology of Old English Poetry: An edition of
Exeter Dean and Chapter MS 3501*, 2 vols (Exeter: University of Exeter Press,
1994), vol. 1, 368.
[36]    Neville, 'The *Exeter Book Riddles*' Precarious Insights into Wooden Artefacts',
130–7.
[37]    Muir, *The Exeter Anthology of Old English Poetry*, 326.

struggle over whether (or when) to bow or not to bow. The Ruthwell Cross says on its north side:

> Buga ...
>       hælda ic ni dorstæ ...

('I [did not] bow ... I dared not bow ...')

and on its south side:

> Saræ ic wæs miþ sorgum gidrœfid,        hnag ...
> miþ strelum giwundad.

('I was sorely troubled with sorrows, [I] bowed down ... wounded by arrows'.)

These words are echoed in the more elaborate lines spoken by the cross in *The Dream of the Rood*.

> hyldan me ne dorste...
> Sare ic wæs mid sorgum gedrefed;        hnag ic hwæðere þam segum
>                                                 to handa
> ead-mod, elne mycle.        Genamon hie þær ælmihtigne God,
> ahofon hine of ðam hefian wite.        Forleton me þa hilderincas
> standan steame bedrifenne;        eall ic wæs mid strælum forwundod.[38]

('I dared not bow ... I was sorely wounded with sorrows I bowed down to the hands of men, humble, with great courage. They took almighty God there, lifted him from that heavy torture. The warriors left me to stand drenched with blood; I was all wounded with arrows'. (lines 45, 59–62)

The cross in both poems dares not bow while Christ lives, but does eventually bow after his death, and in accordance with his will, handing Christ's body down to his followers. (*Hnægan* is the verb used in both poems, a word which Bosworth Toller defines as having the sense of to bow or humble oneself at the command of another.) The bow, on the other hand, is forced to bow or bend (*bugan*) to the will and in the hands of a killer – as it is depicted doing in the Ruthwell Cross archer panel.

---

[38]    Clayton, ed. *Old English Poems of Christ and His Saints*, 162, 164.

Michael Bintley has noted the ultimately regenerative action performed by many of the trees become objects made to serve humans in Anglo-Saxon texts, in particular Exeter Book Riddle 21 (the plough riddle), the *Æcerbot Charm* (a 'charm for unfruitful land'), and *The Dream of the Rood*.[39] The action of the plough creates physical sustenance in the riddle and charm, while that of the cross creates spiritual sustenance in *The Dream of the Rood* and on the Ruthwell Cross.[40] The cross also protects land in numerous rituals and homilies – I will cite here only *Vercelli Book* Homilies XII and XIX,[41] both associated with Rogation days and the blessing of crops, in which a crucifix and/or relics of the Cross are carried in procession in order to protect and regenerate the land. The bow of Riddle 73 also performs regeneration of sorts, as in the longer riddle it may kill but it does so in order to protect its master in war, thereby preserving life. Enemies may have turned it from tree to bow, but enemies now also flee before it. And one could say the same about the bow in Riddles 53 and 46 – both solved not unproblematically as bow. However, the regenerative action of the bow, and through that action its close relationship to the cross as regenerative object, is much clearer and more closely worked out on the Ruthwell Cross, and it is not really necessary to turn to these other and later texts, which simply provide support for a tradition begun, as far as I can discover, within the earlier monument. The arrows from the bow pierce the bodies of Christ and the cross, bringing about the death that leads to resurrection, and a victory over death, both symbolised by the eagle about to take flight towards which the little archer originally shot. And the tree from which the eagle is about to fly bows down, as does the cross in the second half of the runic poem as it hands his body down into the hands of men. The connection between the two is visualised in the similarity between the base of the branch on which the eagle sits and the base from which the vine-scroll rises (Figs 4 and 6).

---

[39]    Michael Bintley, '*Brungen of Bearwe*: Ploughing common furrows in Exeter Book Riddle 21, *The Dream of the Rood*, and the *Æcerbot Charm*', in *Trees and Timber in the Anglo-Saxon World*, ed. Bintley and Shapland, 144–57, esp. 145.
[40]    Bintley, '*Brungen of Bearwe*', 152–4.
[41]    XII for 2nd Rogation Day, XIX for *Dominica ante Rogationum*; see D.G. Scragg, ed., *The Vercelli Homilies*, EETS o. s. 300 (Oxford: EETS, 1992), 227–32, 315–28.

## Back to Earth?

The Ruthwell Cross bowed. Like the tree that became the True Cross it was torn from its roots in the earth, felled, became a dying, ghostly, haunting thing. In 1642, on orders from the General Assembly of the Church of Scotland, the Ruthwell Cross was pulled down and broken into fragments. The Reverend Gavin Young and his congregation had held out against the order of destruction for two years. The cross, it seems, was still a living and valued member of the community. The lower stone was broken in two and partially buried in the floor of Murray's Quire, a funerary chapel that was technically not the property of the church.[42] The upper stone with the archer and eagle was broken into several pieces and, either at this point or sometime during the following hundred years, parts of it were buried or placed under funerary monuments in the churchyard, alongside other members of the local community.

Between the time of its destruction and reconstruction it was visited, drawn and described by numerous antiquaries, all of whom were struck by the paradox of the monumental standing cross that it had once been and the broken stones then before them. Dumfries physician Dr George Archibald described it as having been 'a pillar of stone reaching from the bottom of the church to the roof'.[43] William Nicolson, who had recorded the legend of the cross miraculously growing like a tree to fill the church,[44] also commented on its great height. Nicolson also described some 'little Fragments' of stone sitting on top of the broken shaft, and he discovered some further fragments under some of the table stones (large burial slabs set on pedestals) in the churchyard.[45] The broken stones had been waiting and watching, and were beginning to reassemble. In 1772 Thomas Pennant visited Ruthwell and noted seeing some further fragments (or perhaps they were the same ones Nicolson had seen), including the lower fragment of the John the Baptist panel with the carving of two feet standing on globes, and the upper arm of the cross-head with the eagle on its branch.[46] Further

---

[42]  For an analysis of the wording of the Act in relation to the position of the monument, see Orton and Wood, with Lees, *Fragments of History: Rethinking the Ruthwell and Bewcastle monuments*, 38.

[43]  In Walter MacFarlane, *Geographical Collections*, vol. 3 (Edinburgh: Edinburgh University Press, 1908), 187, 189.

[44]  See above, p. 106.

[45]  Nicolson, 'Bishop Nicolson's Diaries: Part II', 196.

[46]  Thomas Pennant, *A Tour in Scotland and Voyage to the Hebrides 1772* (London: B. White, 1774), vol. 2, 96–8.

fragments of the cross were discovered buried in the churchyard in the nineteenth century by the Reverend Henry Duncan, who began reassembly and reconstruction of the monument. Duncan noted in particular the discovery of the top part of the shaft, the stone that included the archer panel, during the digging of an especially deep grave.[47] Perhaps it was believed that the stone needed to be deeply buried, lest it return to haunt. The cross was reconstructed in the garden of the manse and the capstone with the eagle placed the wrong way round, separating it from the archer firing at him with his arrows. Perhaps this was deliberate. During his 1772 visit, Pennant had recorded yet another legend about the Ruthwell Cross:

> Tradition says that the Church was built over this obelisk long after its erection, and as it was reported to have been transported by angels, it was probably so secured ... least it should take another flight.[48]

Perhaps there was a fear that the eagle might flee the archer's arrows and fly away with the cross, into the air once again.

[47] Duncan, 'An Account of the Remarkable Monument in the Shape of a Cross', 318–19.
[48] Pennant, *A Tour in Scotland and Voyage to the Hebrides 1772*, 96–8.

Slow Manuscripts

# Letter by Letter: Manuscript Transcription and Historical Imagination

## KAREN LOUISE JOLLY

This essay explores the dynamic of combining slow "traditional" methods of scholarship with emerging technological tools, focusing on the digitization of palaeography, as well as exploring the role of historical imagination that comes from slow, deep immersion in the sources. Instead of either passively allowing digital tools to displace good scholarship or, on the other hand, actively resisting technology and throwing the baby out with the bathwater, I argue that medieval scholars are uniquely positioned to leverage these digital tools to demonstrate the relevance of the humanities in a STEM-dominated academic environment, and to reach a wider audience in the general public with the fruits of our studies. In practice, that means engaging in an intentional and continual process of assessing the usefulness and efficiency of the tools we use in our research, writing, and teaching in relation to the values and standards of academic scholarship. But make no mistake: scholarly values are the standard by which we should measure the efficacy of every new technology that comes our way.

These reflections are based on my current research project transcribing a medieval manuscript that has led to some surprising diversions into imagined realms. Durham, Cathedral Library, MS A.IV.19 is an early tenth-century English collectar with materials added in the late tenth century by the community of St. Cuthbert at Chester-le-Street, the home in exile of the Lindisfarne bishopric from 883 prior to its move to Durham in 995. Aldred, the priest who glossed the Lindisfarne Gospels around 950, also glossed in his Northumbrian Old English most of Durham A.IV.19's original collectar and the additions, including his own, dated by his colophon to 970 when he was provost of the community. I am also writing a novel about Aldred. The manuscript transcribing and historical fiction writing interweave in a slow dance with each other.

The tedious business of transcribing, letter by letter, Aldred's Northumbrian Old English gloss of the original collectar in Durham A.IV.19 follows from having already edited the additions to the manuscript in a recent monograph.[1] My purpose now is to create a fully digital edition associating each Latin word with its Old English gloss word to be able to search either direction. In the process of transcribing from the manuscript facsimile, I notice things I would not if I just read it in a print edition. From this close reading of the text is emerging a fictional biography of the manuscript's Northumbrian scribe and glossator Aldred, which is a slow process for a different reason: I need to immerse myself in his world, starting from the manuscript but also sinking myself into the landscape and the material culture, to get closer to his worldview, a process I have been chronicling in the virtual space of a blog.

Like Aldred, I am a slow scholar. I tend to build toward big projects rather than publish a lot of little bits here and there, favoring books over articles, and long articles over short notes and queries. As a full professor, I now have the luxury of spending even more time on projects that might not be evaluated as highly in the academy, such as writing historical fiction. Sadly, with the adjunctification of higher education in the United States (analogous to the corporatization of research in the United Kingdom), this academic freedom – to be expansive, explore, and follow a single path as far as it will go – may be disappearing as the powers-that-be want quantifiable and economically profitable results faster.[2]

Resistance to these trends in academia has coalesced around the concept of "slow scholarship." Since its publication online in 2014, the "Slow Scholarship Manifesto" has generated a lively dialogue, both critiquing its elitism and neoliberal agenda, and expanding its principles to feminist scholarship and political activism.[3] Maggie Berg and Barbara

---

[1]    Karen Louise Jolly, *The Community of St. Cuthbert in the Late Tenth Century: The Chester-le-Street additions to Durham Cathedral Library A.IV.19* (Columbus: The Ohio State University Press, 2012). The critical edition of the manuscript additions is available at the University of Hawai'i at Mānoa's library open access site, ScholarSpace, <https://scholarspace.manoa.hawaii.edu/handle/10125/26967>.

[2]    Simon Head, "How Corporate IT Enslaved Academe," *Chronicle of Higher Education*, June 16, 2014, <http://chronicle.com/article/How-Corporate-IT-Enslaved/147029/?cid=at&utm_source=at&utm_medium=en > (accessed August 1, 2018).

[3]    John Lutz, "Slow Scholarship: A Manifesto," *{slog}: A Slow Blog*, <https://web.uvic.ca/~hist66/slowScholarship/> (accessed August 1, 2018); Heather Mendick, "Social Class, Gender and the Pace of Academic Life: What kind of solution is slow?," *Forum: Qualitative Social Research/Sozialforschung* 15.3 (2014), art. 7 (September 2014), <http://www.qualitative-research.net/index.php/fqs/article/view/2224/3694> (accessed August 1, 2018); Alison Mountz, Anne Bonds, Becky Mansfield, Jenna Loyd, Jennifer Hyndman, Margaret Walton-Roberts, Ranu Basu, Risa Whitson, Roberta Hawkins, Trina Hamilton, and Winifred Curran, "For

K. Seeber, in *The Slow Professor*, summarize the state of North American higher education but also offer some positive ways forward for academics on the ground: fostering the pleasure of learning in the classroom, valuing and rewarding qualitative research that creates new understandings, and restoring scholarly collegiality and community in our hallways.[4]

For someone like myself, a professor at a publicly funded institution, I still have to answer: what value does my scholarship and teaching have, and how do I "sell" that value to legislators, students, and taxpayers? My performance, like most academics, is assessed in three areas: (1) research, productivity measured by quantity and quality of peer-reviewed publications, predominantly articles and books; (2) teaching, mostly undergraduates, the majority of them not in my field, but also preparing graduate students as future teachers and historians; and (3) service, to the department and university, with national or international associations, and through community or public outreach. Reflecting on these three avenues of communication, this essay offers some meta-analysis of what it is I think I am doing as a historian in an increasingly digital landscape dominated by STEM fields of research. My purpose is to contribute to a hermeneutic of slow scholarship as it relates to higher education. I begin with some academic theorizing and then move to some self-examination of a digital medievalist with examples from my current projects, and end by re-imagining history as a discipline and practice in my research, teaching, and service.

## Theory and Higher Education

As teachers, we all complain about our students' inability to do close reading, attributing it to overstimulation from social media and the distractedness of multitasking. Indeed, recent studies of human learning have

---

Slow Scholarship: A feminist politics of resistance through collective action in the neoliberal university," *ACME: An International Journal for Critical Geographies* 14.4 (2015), 1235–59, <https://www.acme-journal.org/index.php/acme/article/view/1058> (accessed August 1, 2018); and "All for Slow Scholarship and Slow Scholarship for All," *University Affairs/Affaires universitaires*, May 9, 2016, <https://www.universityaffairs.ca/opinion/in-my-opinion/slow-scholarship-slow-scholarship/> (accessed August 1, 2018); Beth A. Robertson, "Slow Scholarship as Political Action: The culture of speed and the challenge of inclusion within the academy," *ActiveHistory.ca: History Matters*, June 20, 2016, <http://activehistory.ca/2016/06/slow-scholarship-as-political-action-the-culture-of-speed-and-the-challenge-of-inclusion-within-the-academy/> (accessed August 1, 2018).

[4]    Maggie Berg and Barbara K. Seeber, *The Slow Professor: Challenging the culture of speed in the academy* (Toronto: University of Toronto Press, 2016).

defined a contemporary shift from *deep attention* to *hyper attention*, a seeming generational divide in cognitive modes. Kate Hayles offers these definitions:

> Deep attention ... is characterized by concentrating on a single object for long periods..., ignoring outside stimuli while so engaged, preferring a single information stream, and having a high tolerance for long focus times. Hyper attention, by contrast, is characterized by switching focus rapidly between different tasks, preferring multiple information streams, seeking a high level of stimulation, and having a low tolerance for boredom. ...
>
> Deep attention is superb for solving complex problems represented in a single medium, but it comes at the price of environmental alertness and flexibility of response. Hyper attention excels at negotiating rapidly changing environments in which multiple foci compete for attention; its disadvantage is impatience with focusing for long periods on a non-interactive object.[5]

As Hayles notes, traditional humanities research requires deep attention – or slow scholarship – but now finds itself operating in a world dominated by rapid alternation between tasks.

We all feel this tension in the classroom. Students accustomed to the high stimulation of multimedia and craving rapid shifts of attention are "bored" by the lack of multisensory input, as well as the delay of gratification, in the carefully focused and intense study of a single text or artifact over a long period of time.[6] Some now bemoan the fact that many students currently arriving in college do not know how to write or read cursive and have difficulty hand-writing a two-hour essay exam, raising questions about what gains and losses will occur over time in cognitive functions not yet fully understood by social scientists.[7]

In terms of solutions, one educator urges higher education to promote slow food: rather than store-bought bread, analogous to textbook pabulum, students should make bread from scratch, which I would liken to primary

---

[5]    Kate Hayles, "My Article on Hyper and Deep Attention," *Media Theory for the 21st Century* blog, January 17, 2008, <http://media08.wordpress.com/2008/01/17/my-article-on-hyper-and-deep-attention/> (accessed August 1, 2018).

[6]    See also Hayles's section on reading and brain imaging, which may apply to palaeography

[7]    Stephanie Reese Masson, "The Death of Cursive Writing," *Chronicle of Higher Education Vitae*, December 1, 2016, <https://chroniclevitae.com/news/1625-the-death-of-cursive-writing> (accessed August 1, 2018).

source research that demands concentrated attention to words, and not just rapid skimming and scanning different resources or googling.[8] In other examples, an art history teacher requires her students to contemplate a painting for three full hours at the beginning of their research, a literature professor advocates for being bored while reading novels, and an Anglican priest reflects on John Coltrane's seemingly cacophonic jazz growing on him with repeated listening.[9]

All of those slow techniques promoted in the arts and humanities are attractive to those of us who teach in these fields, but are not necessarily appealing to our students, or, for that matter, their parents, taxpayers, and legislators who question the investment of time and money for activities so seemingly unproductive (in the material sense). The burden, unfortunately, is on academic humanists to articulate the value of deep attention and slow scholarship in relation to the benefits of contemporary hypermedia, as well as recognise the synergy that may develop between these two modes of thought. Medievalists are in a good position to do this work of challenging the assumptions of modernity and technological progress our students and Western societies uncritically and unconsciously accept.[10] Ironically, this is because interdisciplinary medievalists were early adopters of digital technologies to address pre-printing press source issues, while simultaneously being resistant to the modern myths about the pre-modern past.[11]

---

[8] Jennifer Stratton, "We Should Apply the Slow Food Movement to Higher Education," *Chronicle of Higher Education*, February 26, 2014, <http://chronicle. com/blogs/future/2014/02/26/we-should-apply-the-slow-food-movement-to-higher-education/?cid=pm&utm_source=pm&utm_medium=en> (accessed August 1, 2018).

[9] Jennifer L. Roberts, "The Power of Patience," *Harvard Magazine*, November–December 2013, <http://harvardmagazine.com/2013/11/the-power-of-patience> (accessed August 1, 2018); Erik Shonstrom, "People over Pedagogy," *The Chronicle of Higher Education*, July 21, 2014, <http://chronicle.com/article/Ambiguous-Pleasures/147773/?cid=at&utm_source=at&utm_medium=en> (accessed August 1, 2018); Jamie Howison, "God's Mind in that Music," *Collegeville Institute* blog, July 24, 2014, <http://collegevilleinstitute.org/blog/gods-mind-in-that-music/?utm_source=Collegeville+Institute+Mailing+List&utm_medium=email&utm_campaign=02b739ebaf-RSS_EMAIL_CAMPAIGN&utm_term=0_bdd60e05b1-02b739ebaf-76730581> (accessed August 1, 2018).

[10] Jolly, "Bridges and Islands," essay submitted July 2018 for a special issue of *Religion and Literature*.

[11] On text editing, see Bella Millett, "Whatever Happened to Electronic Editing?," 39–54, and Thorlac Turville-Petre, "Editing Electronic Texts," 55–70, and other essays in *Probable Truth: Editing Medieval Texts from Britain in the Twenty-First Century*, ed. Vincent Gillespie and Anne Hudson (Turnhout:

A Digital Medievalist

For medieval historians, slow scholarship and deep attention are closely
tied to the nature of our textual sources: manuscripts as artefacts, not
just texts transmitted any which way. Medieval texts were done by hand,
painstakingly slowly, by scribes who were in a very real sense creating a
unique artefact, a one-off. Why do we think we could understand their
work without engaging in the same painstaking and slow process of deci-
phering the manuscript page? In that sense, early modern palaeographers
had an advantage over us: they labored in the archives with pen and paper
or notecards, rather than laptops, cameras, and scanners. Early modern
palaeographers, like Humphrey Wanley, practiced their own imitation
of the scribal hands they studied, thereby becoming deeply immersed in
the scribal culture of Anglo-Saxon manuscripts.[12] Inspired by an innovative workshop bringing together calligraphers and palaeographers, I have
begun to imitate Aldred's scribal handiwork, although my insular minuscule is quite rudimentary.[13]

On the other hand, nostalgia for the old days of archival work does
not mean we should be Luddites and eschew technology. Wanley and his
generation would be entranced with our ability to visualise and analyse
scribal hands using digital scanning, not to mention the democratizing of
the archive provided by the (usually free) access to high resolution images
of rare manuscripts and the ability to "scientifically" measure and compare
color, nib width, and pen strokes of different scribes side by side. Rather,
we need to understand what these tools can do for us while maintaining
the deep attention to the textual artefact that slow scholarship requires.

My encounters with digitisation go back to the dawn of the personal
computer in the early 1980s, so I have had time to witness and reflect
on its implications. When I was in graduate school researching aspects of
Anglo-Saxon pastoral care for my dissertation on Anglo-Saxon charms, two
of my fellow graduate students at the University of California at Santa
Barbara had embarked on a massive project to create the first iteration

---

Brepols, 2013). On the modern construction of the medieval, see Kathleen Davis,
*Periodization and Sovereignty: How ideas of feudalism and secularization govern the
politics of time* (Philadelphia, PA: University of Pennsylvania Press, 2008).

[12]    Jolly, *Community of St. Cuthbert*, 88–9.

[13]    University of Iowa Obermann Center for Advanced Studies Summer 2008
Research Seminar, Medieval Manuscript Studies and Contemporary Book Arts:
Extreme Materialist Readings of Medieval Books; see the resulting publication
*Scraped, Stroked, and Bound: Materially engaged readings of medieval manuscripts,*
ed. Jon Wilcox (Turnhout: Brepols, 2013).

of a Domesday Book database.[14] Domesday Book is a unique as well as problematic demographic source, especially on the distribution of churches and priests in late Anglo-Saxon England. I was quite happy to rely on the statistics developed by previous scholars, but Robin Fleming urged me to go through Domesday Book myself to count up all the churches and priests. So I did, using 3" x 5" cards that I still haven't the heart to throw away; then I entered the information into my first-generation IBM PC and sorted the data using a program custom-written by my engineer husband. Meanwhile, Robin and Katie Mack were working on setting up the Domesday Book database. First, though, they needed to have all the categories in place before the data could be entered. Infamously, there is one ditch digger, a *fossarius*, in Domesday Book, so the database had to have a column for that one instance (Robin and Katie even had lab coats with *fossarius* on them, an appropriate metaphor for what they were doing). This example demonstrates that before you can sort data you have to know what you are looking for, which means you have to have already read it. So much for hyper-attentive data mining without attentive deep reading.

Instead, we need a mindful process to marry this new technology to our slow scholarship methods inductively as well as deductively. Historians like to think of themselves as inductive thinkers. They explore what is there trotting, fox-like, down different paths, without many preconceptions about where they will lead, looking for patterns or oddities.[15] Consequently, most historians are wary of social science deductive hypothesizing, even though they may adopt certain theories as explanatory models. In reality, most historical research is a complex process of moving between text and theory, source and thought. Nonetheless, historians claim, in reaction to the social sciences model-building, that we need to see what is there first, before imposing definitions and patterns. Indeed, many historians shy away from general rules and prefer oddities, unique circumstances, things that do not fit.[16] We teach our students to read a lot, to slow down and look for interesting things, a bit like gold-mining, except that one person's dross is another person's gold.

---

[14]   Robin Fleming, now at Boston College, and Katherine Mack (†). Sadly, I learned that Katie passed away after a long battle with cancer while I was initially preparing the conference presentation in 2014 on which this essay is based.

[15]   Isaiah Berlin, *The Hedgehog and the Fox: An essay on Tolstoy's view of history* (London: Weidenfeld & Nicolson, 1967).

[16]   Its most extreme form is microhistory as propounded by Carlo Ginzburg; see *Microhistory and the Lost Peoples of Europe*, ed. Edward Muir and Guido Ruggiero, trans. Eren Branch (Baltimore, MD: Johns Hopkins University Press, 1991).

This is precisely how I found myself drawn to Aldred and his glosses in Durham A.IV.19. Aldred is an oddity in a number of ways: in the texts he copied, including five unusual prayers for clearing birds from the field; for his seemingly archaic scribal hand and his distinctively Northumbrian Old English; and in his fulsome yet mysterious colophons in Durham A.IV.19 and the Lindisfarne Gospels. Perhaps Aldred is unique, not a typical Northumbrian scribe, and therefore not a good guide to Northumbria's contribution to English linguistic history, although his glosses make up a disproportionate number of our Northumbrian Old English dictionary entries. What I am finding as I transcribe his glosses from the manuscript facsimile into my computer is how he thinks about words and language, which may be idiosyncratic but still reflect something of his time and place.

I offer here two examples gleaned from my transcriptions of Aldred's glosses to the capitula (Bible chapter readings) in Durham A.IV.19 that generated speculative blog posts and fodder for my novel.[17] In both, Aldred's "misglossing" reveals aspects of brotherly relations in a religious community that I would have otherwise missed if I had not been moving so slowly.

### Faith and Love

In the first example, Aldred has a seemingly unique notion of Latin *fides*, a word we normally associate with the religious sense of belief and with the social sense of being loyal.[18] We today, and even Aldred's contemporaries, would not usually translate *fides* as "love," but Aldred does. He glossed the capitula from 1 Cor. 13:13, "Now however remain faith, hope, love, these three; but the greater of these is love," in this way:

---

[17]    All transcriptions from *Durham Priory Library Recreated* <https:// www. durhampriory.ac.uk/> (accessed August 1, 2018). Durham, Cathedral Library, MS A.IV.19 (hereafter referred to as Durham A.IV.19), <https://iiif.durham.ac.uk/ index.html?manifest=t2m0p096691f> (accessed August 1, 2018). See also the facsimile edition, *The Durham Ritual*, ed. T.J. Brown, Early English Manuscripts in Facsimile 16 (Copenhagen: Rosenkilde & Bagger, 1969). For a recent edition of the Latin, see *The Durham Collectar*, ed. Alicea Corrêa, Henry Bradshaw Society 107 (London: Boydell Press for the Henry Bradshaw Society, 1992), and for the Latin with Old English gloss, see *Rituale ecclesiae Dunelmensis: The Durham Collectar*, ed. U. Lindelöf with introduction by A. Hamilton Thompson, Surtees Society 140 (London: Andrews for the Surtees Society, 1927).

[18]    Jolly, "Faith, Hope, and Love," *Revealing Words* blog, <http://litteramepandat.wordpress.com/2013/05/29/faith-hope-and-love/> (accessed August 1, 2018).

*broð' nv wvt' wvnað lvfv [ł gileafa] hyht godes lvfv*
1 Fr*atre*s nunc autem manent fides spes caritas
*ðri' [o] ðasv' mara wvt' ðisra is broðer lvfv*
2 tria haec. maior aute*m* [h]oru*m* est caritas.[19]

The addition of *Fratres* ("brothers") at the opening is the way these capitula for Septuagesima and Sexagesima are all introduced in the original collectar. The vocative address to brothers establishes the context for Aldred's thinking about this verse: it highlights the relationships between members of a religious community, such as the one to which Aldred belonged at Chester-le-Street and for whom he was glossing this collectar.

Above *fides*, Aldred first wrote *lufu*, then added later above it *vel gileafa*: love, or belief.

Athough *lufu* is the Old English root for the modern word love, we should be careful to see a different spectrum of meaning and valence than our view of love. Nonetheless, it is an unusual way to translate Latin *fides* not found outside of Aldred's glosses anywhere else in the rest of the Old English corpus. Nor is this the only place Aldred glossed *fides* with *lufu*. Five other instances of Aldred glossing *lufu* on *fides* occur in the main collecatar of Durham A.IV.19.[20] Likewise in his gloss to the Lindisfarne Gospels, he uses *lufu* for *fides* in at least eight places, two with a *vel [ge] leafa*, all of which are in introductory materials, not the Gospel texts themselves.[21] More typically in line with other Old English glossators,

---

[19]   Durham A.IV.19, fol. 3v, lines 1–2. Abbreviations marked with a single quote in Old English: *broð'* nom. pl. could be *brothor, brother, brothro, brothru*; *wut* = *witodlic*; *thri* has "o" after with deletion dots above and below; *thasv'* also may have deletion marks about the final "v." Aldred added *[ł gileafa]* above *lvfv* in line 1, as discussed below, and added the initial « h » to *horum* in line 2.

[20]   Durham A.IV.19, fols 1r18, 18v17, 24r16, 28v3, and 44v10.

[21]   London, British Library, Cotton MS Nero D.IV <http://www.bl.uk/manuscripts/Viewer.aspx?ref=cotton_ms_nero_d_iv_fs001r> (accessed August 1, 2018); for contents, see Michelle P. Brown, *The Lindisfarne Gospels: Society, spirituality and the scribe* (London: British Library, 2003), Appendix 2 (CD-rom). The two with *vel [ge]leafa* are: fol. 21vb24, in the prefatory Matthew Capitula Lectionum Incipit, part of a reference to the Canaanite mother's love or belief for the healing of her demoniac daughter; and at fol. 90va6, closely followed at fol. 90va9 by *to lufo* glossing *fidei*, in a curious passage in the Mark prologue about how the evangelist *post fidem* amputated his own thumb to avoid the priesthood in which Aldred's gloss misapprehends both *amputare* and *pollex* (for the Latin text and translation, see Ben C. Smith, "The Latin Prologues," *Text Excavation*, <http://textexcavation.com/latinprologues.html> (accessed August 1, 2018). The other instances of *lufu* glossing *fides* are: at fol. 3vb13, in Jerome's *Nouum Opus*; at fol. 6vb2, in Jerome's *Plures Fuisse*; and in Matthew's Argumentum, at fol. 18va21,

Aldred does use Old English *lufu* as a gloss to Latin *caritas, amor,* or *dilectio,* so he clearly understands *lufu* in what we would consider the more usual meaning of love. What is unique to Aldred here is his understanding of the word *fides* and its range of meaning, from love to belief.

In the case of Durham A.IV.19, fol. 3, the addition above the line of *vel gileafa* providing the alternative belief to the love gloss of *fides,* appears to be a second stage of glossing reacting to the context of the Bible verse. That is, *lufu* was his first response to the word *fides,* glossing word for word without consideration of the rest of the phrase (although assuredly this passage would be familiar enough for him to anticipate the redundancy). As he read forward and encountered *caritas* (twice), he needed to find a way of distinguishing *fides* from *caritas* in Old English.

In my palaeographic reconstruction of his process, Aldred does three things to make sense of the three loves he ends up with in his gloss of this passage, although in what order is unknown. First, as he moved forward after *fides* glossed only with *lufu,* he encounters *caritas,* as the third virtue in the list of faith, hope, and love, and distinguishes it from *fides lufu* by glossing it with *godes lufu* ("God's love").[22] On the next line, he distinguishes the second *caritas* as *broðer lufu* ("brotherly love"), echoing the invocation of brothers at the outset. At some point, he goes back and adds *vel gileafa* to the *lufu* gloss of *fides* to distinguish it from *caritas,* both *godes lufu* and *broðer lufu.* This triad connects God's love to, on the one hand, faithful love and on the other, to brotherly love, significantly presented here as the greater love.

In an analogous instance, Aldred glossed Latin *credere* ("to believe"), usually associated with creedal belief, with the verb love:[23]

> *sel ciricae ðinre ve bid' 7 lvfia þ'te lvfade 7 bodia þ' gilærde*
> da ecclesiae tuae quesumus et amare quod credidit, et predicare
>     quod docuit.        Per.[24]

where *credendi fide* is glossed with *leafes lufu,* at fol. 18vb15, and at fol. 19ra20. These examples are from prefatory material to Matthew and Mark, and the earlier Jerome materials, none from later in the manuscript.

22    He runs into a similar difficulty later in the manuscript at fol. 44v10, where he glosses *fidei caritatisque* with *lvfv' 7 godes lvfv.*

23    Jolly, "Thought and Belief," Revealing Words blog, June 11, 2013, <http://litteramepandat.wordpress.com/2013/06/11/thought-and-belief/> (accessed August 1, 2018). In the hot iron ordeal, at fol. 54v10, Aldred glosses *catholicam* with *gileafful.*

24    Durham A.IV.19, fol. 23r6-9. "Grant your church, we pray, to love what he [John] believed, and to preach what he taught."

This Latin prayer for the celebration of the birth of St. John the Evangelist on 27 December asks that God through St. John grant the church to love (*amare*) what he, that is John, believed (*credidit*) and preach what he taught. However, Aldred glosses it to "love what he *loved* (*lvfade*) and preach what he taught." To love what your lord loves sounds strikingly similar to fidelity oaths in a secular context, where love is tied to loyalty and obedience. This link between love and obedience is consonant with the Christian tradition as well: "if you love me, keep my commandments," Jesus taught (John 14:15). This gloss reflects a core value in monastic identity, as Katherine O'Brien O'Keeffe has admirably shown in her book *Stealing Obedience*, that monastic communities are built around obedience.[25] Whether or to what degree Aldred's community at Chester-le-Street was "monastic" in character or practice (more likely a secular collegiate foundation), this gloss suggests a concern for brotherly love in community.

Clearly these glosses constitute more commentary than translation, despite the word-by-word format and lack of marginal annotations of the type normally associated with commentary. Seen as commentary, Aldred's glosses offer further insight into an early medieval religious mentality that we might otherwise dismiss as merely translating known texts, and sometimes poorly at that. Whether or not Aldred is correct or incorrect in his gloss translation becomes irrelevant when our interest is in seeing how his mind works bilingually. What Aldred's gloss reveals in the context of his religious community, is how at least he understood *lufu* as meaning both faith and love, and vice versa, thought of faith as involving love as well as belief.

## Self-Control

In the second case of a possible Aldredism in Durham A.IV.19, he "corrects" the Latin of the original collectar (Scribe O's work) while glossing it. Aldred is glossing a series of Bible verse incipits used in the daily round of prayers. This particular set, as with the previous example, all start with *Fratres*, brothers, and come from Paul's letters in the New Testament. In this case it is a passage from Colossians 3:12–13.

[25]  Jolly, "Obedience," *Revealing Words* blog, June 6, 2013, <http://litteramepan-dat.wordpress.com/2013/06/06/obedience/> (accessed August 1, 2018); Katherine O'Brien O'Keeffe, *Stealing Obedience: Narratives of agency and identity in later Anglo-Saxon England* (Toronto: University of Toronto Press, 2012).

*broð' giwoedes [vel] ivih svoelce gicoreno godes hælgo 7 gileafo*
Fr*atre*s. induite uos sicut electi d*e*i sanc*ti* et dilecti uis-

*innaðo miltheartniss'es weldonis' [vel] rv'mod' eðmodnise*
cera misericordiae. benignitate*m* humilitatem

*gimetfæstnis' giðyld vnderbearað bitvien*
modestia*m*. patientiam. subportantes inuicem

*7 onwældað ivh seolfv'*
et do[:mi]nantes uobismetipsis.[26]

The Douay–Rheims (1899 American edition) translation is "Put ye on
therefore, as the elect of God, holy, and beloved, the bowels of mercy,
benignity, humility, modesty, patience: Bearing with one another, and
forgiving one another." But in the last phrase, Aldred has altered the original Latin *donantes* ("forgiving" in this context) by inserting "mi" above
to make *dominantes*, literally "dominating" one another! He does it quite
deliberately, using a colon insertion mark between the "o" and the "n"
and writing the "mi" in large letters to match the original scribe's style,
albeit in his red glossing ink.

This seems a rather rude understanding of his relationship with his
brothers in the community but could indicate the kind of control an
abbot or provost should have over the members. Still, it doesn't seem to
match the "bowels of mercy" and bearing with one another that Paul calls
for in this passage.

It might seem, therefore, that Aldred does not know the rest of the
verse omitted in the capitula, which clarifies *donantes* as reciprocal for-
giveness in imitation of Christ: "if any have a complaint against another:
even as the Lord hath forgiven you, so do you also."[27] However, the
Old English gloss Aldred places over *dominantes* is *onwældað ivh seolfvm*
("control yourself"), which suggests that he may have understood the
phrase to refer to the monastic virtue of self-control. In the absence of the
rest of the verse about complaints against each other and forgiving as God
forgives, Aldred may have focused on the self-control necessary to bear
one another's burdens in his community. *Donantes* with its root meaning

---

[26]    Durham A.IV.19 fol. 6v16–19. Jolly, "Control Yourselves!," *Revealing Words*
blog, September 22, 2013, <http://litteramepandat.wordpress.com/2013/09/22/
control-yourselves/> (accessed August 1, 2018).
[27]    Vulgate Latin: *si quis adversus aliquem habet querellam sicut et Dominus
donavit vobis ita et vos.*

*to give* didn't work for him or the train of thought set in motion by the earlier part of the verse, so he changed the Latin text of the Scripture.

Combined with the previous example, just three folios earlier, these anomalies suggest that Aldred is not just a lone glossator but is actively reflecting on the Biblical text in community, possibly while conversing with other members of the Chester-le-Street clergy or novices. Because the only thing usually visible to us is the text as the handiwork of a scribe, we often fail to imagine the other people present, the conversations taking place, or the gestures and behaviors performed.

## Imagining History

What that conversation between Aldred and his brothers might have been like is unknowable to the historian but can be imagined by the novelist. My fictionalizing started with a different passage in Durham A.IV.19, where Aldred both corrected and glossed the rather poor handiwork of Scribe B.[28] As I transcribed letter by letter – and even tried to imitate Scribe B's incompetent letter formations (mine were worse), I noticed that Scribe B had responded to some of Aldred's corrections in subsequent lines, which means they were working simultaneously, master and pupil. So I began to imagine them talking to each other about the writing process as well as the text. I crossed a line when I began to call Scribe B, "Bert," short for Berctwin I decided. I wrote a short story about the encounter, visible on the manuscript page, between Aldred and Bert.

Next, I began taking other texts that Aldred wrote himself or glossed and tried to imagine situations in which the text might be meaningful. At first, I did not stray far from the scriptorium where he might discuss a nugget of theology with a novice, but then I started to put him out in the landscape, at first sticking with texts he knew and places he was known to have been. For example, we know he was in Wessex on August 10, 970 because he tells us in his colophon to Durham A.IV.19 that he was at Oakley just south of Woodyates on St. Lawrence's feast on Wodensday when the moon was five nights old.[29] After GoogleEarthing the coordinates (50° 58' N x 1° 58' W), I went there and tramped around the barrow downs, trying to ignore later developments such as rabbit holes and tree plantations. After that, I began to imagine Aldred in other places he might have gone – Cumbria, Lindisfarne, Iona – and texts he might have read.

---

[28] Durham A.IV.19, fol. 61r11–22; see Jolly, *Community of St. Cuthbert*, 155–62.
[29] Durham A.IV.19, fol. 84r; see Jolly, *Community of St. Cuthbert*, 1, 6–9.

Going even further afield, I began to introduce materials I happened to be reading: after receiving at about the same time the new edition of the Old English Boethius and the Battle of Brunanburh Casebook, I imagined Aldred as a young man at the battle in 937 reading the Old English Boethius and reflecting on the direction of his life.[30]

Still, even with all of these imagined scenarios, I stay tethered to the Aldred I know from his gloss translations in Durham A.IV.19 and the Lindisfarne Gospels. At the same time that I may be working on the logistics of time, place, and feeling for a historical novel, I sit at the computer and transcribe Aldred's gloss to the collectar from the facsimile. When I come across odd glosses like the examples here and on my blog, they add to the storehouse of my knowledge about Aldred's way of thinking about himself and his community. Thus, transcribing the gloss is a way into his mental landscape I can use to write a story that might allow modern readers a glimmering of a very different worldview.

What also slows me down and keeps me grounded in medieval material culture is practicing palaeography by copying Aldred's script, as well as developing my own insular minuscule hand. Although I have semi-authentic reproduction materials (quill, oak gall ink, parchment), I generally use a felt-tipped calligraphy pen on paper, easier and cheaper. I find it relaxing, but also insightful. In one instance, copying a word added to the original Latin allowed me to identify Aldred as the scribe who did it, based on the nib angle; and in another, playing with the remnants of an erased letter helped me identify it as an "x."[31] My many scribal mistakes also remind me of how skillful scribes like Aldred were (I am more like Scribe B). The difficulties of this painstaking work have caused me to reflect on the complex relationship between letter forms and words, the eye–hand–brain connection of crafstmanship that requires 10,000 hours of apprenticeship to perfect.[32]

---

[30]   *The Old English Boethius*, ed. and trans. Susan Irvine and Malcolm R. Godden (Cambridge, MA: Harvard University Press, 2012); *The Battle of Brunanburh: A casebook*, ed. Michael Livingston (Exeter: University of Exeter Press, 2011).

[31]   Jolly, "Nunc," *Revealing Words* blog, November 4, 2014, <https://litteramepandat.wordpress.com/2014/11/04/nunc/> (accessed August 1, 2018); and "Hungering and Thirsting," February 2, 2015, <https://litteramepandat.wordpress.com/2015/02/16/hungering-and-thirsting/> (accessed August 1, 2018).

[32]   See Jolly, "Dismembering and Reconstructing Durham Cathedral Library A.IV.19," in *Scraped, Stroked, and Bound*, ed. Wilcox, 177–200; R. Sennett, *The Craftsman* (New Haven, CT: Yale University Press, 2008). As my children's violin teacher used to say, quoting Dr. Shin'ichi Suzuki, 'ten times knowledge, ten thousand times ability'.

## Research, Teaching, and Service

In my calling as a slow professor, how do I transfer these insights and skills to the next generation? At present, I am leveraging the new multimedia environment to promote and communicate my "slow" thinking in three ways, in the tenurable categories of research, teaching, and service.

First, I am becoming a "digital humanist," taking advantage of the increasing availability of manuscript images online and my university's eagerness to support emerging technologies. The ability to sit in my office in Hawai'i and pull up high-resolution images of manuscripts – for free – from archives such as the British Library, the Parker Library (Corpus Christi College, Cambridge), and Durham Priory, is truly an astounding change from even five years ago when I would be peering at black and white facsimiles in print or on microfilm, many of them available only through InterLibrary Loan, or scraping together enough funding to cover a research trip to the archives almost halfway around the world. Building on this digitization, paleographic analysis for comparing scribal hands is now possible with projects like DigiPal and the Mirador viewer (IIIF) protocol.[33] The quality of these images does not completely eliminate the need to see the manuscript in person, in three dimensions. For example, what looked like a stray ink mark turned out to be a hole from an erasure on the verso by another scribe, with a bit of hanging chad.[34] In other instances, I might need to check the foliation and binding to look for missing folios or cut pages. Nonetheless, the digital images reduce by far the needless handling of rare and sometimes fragile manuscripts, as well as speed up my research without the expense and time of travel.

Even while humanists decry the decline in research support in favor of STEM, they can also leverage the technological emphasis to make the humanities more visible on their campuses. As a participant in my university's interdisciplinary Digital Arts and Humanities Initiative, I help demonstrate the value of humanities research, even though my field of early medieval European history is considered marginal at best to the university's stated "areas of excellence." My colleague David Goldberg in American Studies, who analyzes contemporary graffiti and hip hop,

---

[33] See *DigiPal: Digital Resource and Database of Manuscripts, Palaeography and Diplomatic* (London, 2011–14), <http://www.digipal.eu/> (accessed August 1, 2018); Project Mirador, <https://github.com/ProjectMirador/mirador> (accessed August 1, 2018); IIIF (International Image Interoperability Framework) <http://iiif.io/about/> (accessed August 1, 2018).

[34] Durham A.IV.19, fol. 84rv, see Jolly, *Community of St. Cuthbert*, 79–80.

designed a software program for turning my bilingual text transcriptions from Aldred's glosses into a searchable two-way glossary. That bit of software is now being adapted by scholars mining the vast and barely tapped Hawaiian-language archives currently undergoing digitisation.[35] The synergy between American pop culture, Hawaiian language, and Anglo-Saxon history only happens serendipitously when we have academic environments that foster these personal encounters and scholarly conversations, as Berg and Seeber argued.

Second, my teaching has gradually transformed into something much more interactive, spontaneous, and hands-on, and surprisingly, sometimes more like a medieval pedagogical environment. I have experimented with technologies in flipped classrooms and online teaching, as well as old-fashioned seminar-style discussions with no multimedia. I assign obscure medieval philosophers, make students act out parts from a primary source, and shamelessly play devil's advocate to challenge their assumptions. I let them show me what they are reading and watching – anime, games, poems, movies. Even if it is completely alien to me, everything is fodder for analysis and reflection. To complement my students' hyper-attentive texting skills and develop their deep attention to words, I slow them down by going medieval. In one Honors seminar, I focused on the theories of the Trivium using, among other things, Plato, Boethius, Antoine de Saint-Exupéry, Tolkien, Old English texts with parallel translations by modern poets, and a set of calligraphy pens.[36] Electronics off, we read aloud stories and poems, practiced medieval scripts, and listened to medieval music. Their final "braided essays" combined their own reading experiences with critical analysis of medieval ways of thinking. No matter what the technology or lack thereof, the goal is getting students to think deeply about what matters to the human condition. And sometimes I have the privilege of seeing the light bulb go on over a student's head, or read an essay that provokes me to think more deeply.

Third, I am reaching a wider public with my blog, a form of thinking in progress in lieu of incremental publication.[37] One of the reflective critiques of slow scholarship, by Heather Mendick, pointed out the way social media platforms like blogging or Twitter speed up the transition

---

[35]    See the Papakilo Database, Office of Hawaiian Affairs, <https://www.papaki-lodatabase.com/> (accessed August 1, 2018).

[36]    *The Word Exchange: Anglo-Saxon poems in translation*, ed. Greg Delanty and Michael Matto (New York: W.W. Norton, 2011).

[37]    Jolly, "About," *Revealing Words* blog, January 2012 <https://litteramepandat. wordpress.com/about/> (accessed August 1, 2018).

from a descriptive mode to an analytic mode, and wondered, "Which lines of flight does the internet open up for academic work and which close down?"[38] She acknowledges that slow scholarship is a useful way of inhibiting the jump to hasty interpretations, a warning more generally needed in our rapid-fire social media environment.[39] Eschewing Facebook and Twitter, I find the blog environment offers that in between space for reflection prior to publication, similar to a conference venue. I can start from the descriptive mode and piecemeal lay out the process of analysis, without needing to refine it into a definitive argument, as would be required in a peer-reviewed published article. Blogging is also a good cure for writer's block and procrastination: it forces me to put into words what I am trying to say and then let it simmer for a bit before I move it into something formal. In the context of historical fiction, blogging allows me to explore the landscape and culture before I try to translate that into fiction, whereas before I would just publish the scholarly analysis. In this way, the fruits of my slow scholarship may eventually satisfy a public thirst for history in a form they can imbibe.

[38]   Mendick, "Social Class, Gender and the Pace of Academic Life," [9].
[39]   See Jaron Lanier, *Ten Arguments for Deleting Your Social Media Accounts Right Now* (New York: Henry Holt, 2018).

# Slow Digitisation and the Battle of the Books

## ANDREW PRESCOTT

*The battle facing the books today has nothing to do with arguments between Plato and Aristotle or Paganism and Christianity: it has to do with the survival of the books themselves.*

Robin Alston

Among the colleagues during the twenty years I worked at the British Library who profoundly influenced me was the historian of the English language, bibliographer and librarian, Robin Alston (1933–2011).[1] Robin's great scholarly achievement was his twenty-volume *Bibliography of the English Language from the Invention of Printing to the Year 1800*,[2] but the range of his achievements and interests stretched far beyond this. While he was a lecturer at the University of Leeds, he founded Scolar Press to provide cheap facsimiles of historical and literary texts for his students. As editor-in-chief of the Eighteenth Century Short Title Catalogue, which afterwards became the English Short Title Catalogue or ESTC, Robin profoundly influenced the way in which we use printed books from the hand press period. Robin's insistence that this new catalogue should be machine readable and his energy in driving forward the ESTC laid the foundations of such current digital resources as Early English Books Online and Eighteenth-Century Collections Online. Robin was one of the pioneers who shaped the modern digital research environment for humanities scholars.

In 1990, Robin was appointed Professor of Library and Information Studies at University College London, and he gave his inaugural lecture at UCL, entitled 'The Battle of the Books', on 16 February 1993. I attended, with many others from the British Library.[3] The atmosphere was electric.

---

[1] Obituary by Stephen Green, The Guardian, 2 October 2011: https://www.theguardian.com/books/2011/oct/02/robin-alston-obituary (accessed 12 November 2018).

[2] R. Alston, *A Bibliography of the English Language from the Invention of Printing to the Year 1800: A systematic record of writings on English, and on other languages in English, based on the collections of the principal libraries of the world* (20 vols, Leeds: E.J. Arnold, 1965–2011).

[3] Sadly, this lecture was never published, but the text is available in a posting by Robin to the Humanist online discussion group, 7.176, 10 September 1993,

Robin was known as a charismatic, entertaining and thought-provoking lecturer who provided remarkable insights into current and future developments. He did not fail on this occasion. Robin took his starting point Jonathan Swift's satire, *A Full and True Account of the Battle Fought Last Friday between the Ancient and the Modern Books in St James's Library*, appended to the *Tale of a Tub* (1704). Swift imagined the books in the Royal Library joining in the conflict between those who revered classical learning and those who stressed the need for up-to-date modern learning. Swift described solitary volumes of classical learning being threatened by the massed ranks of thousands of modern books.

For Robin, Swift's satire encapsulated the dangers confronting librarianship as the web revolution was beginning. I remember that Robin's lecture was the first time I heard the words 'internet surfing', and many of the audience were astonished to learn that there were people who could earn a living from surfing databases. Robin was at the forefront of persuading librarians and bibliographers that they should exploit the potential of new forms of information technology, but on this occasion he sounded an alarm bell. Robin painted a picture of powerful commercial interests persuading libraries to invest heavily in computers that may not have been needed. He warned of the dangers of the creation of hypermarkets of information. 'The notion that knowledge can prosper by creating vast knowledge warehouses based on the hypermarket model – you can buy it if you can find it – is sheer fantasy as well as being intellectually suspect,' Robin declared. While emphasising how the availability of journal articles and new publications over networks could aid the cause of the moderns by making recent scholarship more accessible, Robin pointed out the risks of forgetting how the exploration of the works of the ancients in rare books and manuscripts was complex and time-consuming and that, for all the great electronic resources then becoming available, there were still vast quantities of printed and manuscript material inaccessible to the computer.

The contemporary battle of the books as described by Alston is a war between information and knowledge. It is a battle between moderns who propose that, by digitising every scrap of vellum and paper, all human understanding will become available, and ancients who argue that knowledge is gained by an extended intellectual journey in search of understanding about humanity. It is a battle between those who worship speed and efficiency and those who want to proceed more slowly and haphazardly. Robin described how science has improved the human condition, but pointed out how

http://lists.village.virginia.edu/lists_archive/Humanist/v07/0175.html (accessed 12 November 2018). All quotes from Robin's lecture are from this copy.

the discoveries which have contributed to this have also had malign consequences: none more malign, I think, than the notion that knowledge is amenable to mechanical transference. Information without doubt, but knowledge decidedly not.

Robin graphically described the commercial and political forces that he believed were driving these processes:

> The temptation to transform research libraries into commercially driven surfing is already in evidence and conforms politically to the Friedman doctrine which holds that the notion of public service is obsolete and that libraries and education must be paid for by users or they will have to do without.

It was for these reasons that Robin argued that the modern battle of the books was not simply about forms of knowledge but was also a battle for the survival of the books themselves. For Robin, it was vital for librarians to develop new skills that blended ancient and modern techniques if they were to ensure that libraries were not replaced by new commercial networks and the superannuated books discarded.

Robin's lecture was remarkably prescient, and many of the dangers he foresaw twenty-five years ago are now urgent and daily threats. Robin's fear that powerful commercial interests would monopolise human culture by mass digitisation, perhaps abetted by librarians anxious to safeguard their own institutions, anticipated the appearance of Google Books and the way in which family history companies such as Ancestry and Findmypast have effectively privatised large swathes of historical records. Robin would have been horrified by the arbitrary way in which some librarians use the availability of digital surrogates to restrict access to original books and manuscripts, restricting the ability of scholars to investigate such physical features as watermarks or quiring structures. He would have been dismayed by the poor presentation in online packages such as Eighteenth-Century Collections Online of such features as the illustrations of eighteenth-century books. Robin also anticipated the rise of the MOOC in teaching and warned that digital access to course materials could be used as a means of avoiding the high costs of face-to-face teaching.

The modern battle of the books is between those moderns who see the value of books and manuscripts in their informational content and the ancients who prefer more slowly to explore the structure and character of books and manuscripts, using digital tools to investigate them more deeply. For the moderns, the important requirement is to undertake as much digitisation as quickly as possible; for the ancients, the value of digitisation is in its ability to provide a variety of tools that facilitate highly detailed bibliographic analysis. The moderns cherish the ability of the computer to facilitate mass searching and distant reading; the ancients admire the way in which the computer enables them to go deeper and analyse with finer and finer degrees of granularity. Of course, it is not helpful to present these two approaches as completely antithetical. For example, the way in which the *Global Currents* project at Stanford and Groningen Universities automatically retrieves certain manuscript features such as *litterae notabiliores* and rubrics to facilitate comparison of scribal practice across a large number of twelfth-century manuscripts in the Parker Library at Corpus Christi College Cambridge may be seen at one level as using techniques of mass digitisation, but these methods are used to facilitate a detailed investigation of scribal behaviour, corresponding to the kind of bibliographic approach that Alston identified with the ancients.[4] Nevertheless, we can clearly discern a difference between those who would emphasise the managerial and efficiency gains of digitisation and those who would enlist digital tools in support of finer-grained and slower forms of analysis.

Robin Alston's 'Battle of the Books' was a warning against the dangers of mass digitisation. In a similar vein, in a recent article for *Archive Journal*, Lorna Hughes and I have argued for 'slow digitisation'.[5] We commented that:

> Too often, digitisation is treated as a form of colour microfilm, thereby offering distorted views of the manuscript and making it appear to be a simpler and more stable object than it really is. Digitisation provides a constantly expanding toolbox for probing and analysing manuscripts that goes beyond simple colour imaging. Like archaeological artefacts, manuscripts should be explored gradually, using a variety of technical aids and methods, building a multifaceted digital archive of the manuscript.

We defined 'slow digitisation' as follows:

> Just as there is a movement for 'slow food', so might we conceive of developing a movement advocating 'slow digitisation', in which rapid access is less important than the use of technological and other tools to

---

[4]   https://globalcurrents.stanford.edu/ (accessed 20 November 2018).
[5]   Andrew Prescott and Lorna Hughes, 'Why Do We Digitize? The case for slow digitization', *Archive Journal*, September 2018, http://www.archivejournal.net/essays/why-do-we-digitize-the-case-for-slow-digitization/ (accessed 12 November 2018).

gradually excavate the complex layers that make up each manuscript. By 'slow digitisation' we mean not just the delivery of high-resolution digital images as a form of 'digital photocopying', where a single image capture of each page of a manuscript is presented as the definitive view of the folio as an object, but the use of advanced imaging techniques, including 3-D, RTI, and hyperspectral imaging – as well as specialised images such as those captured by raking light from angles other than a camera held directly above a flattened leaf. These two approaches – slow and mass digitisation – are by no means inimical, but they need to be held in balance.

In advocating for 'slow digitisation', Lorna and I were chiefly motivated by a concern that the full possibilities of digital imaging are not being exploited by libraries and archives, but there are also parallels between our call for 'slow digitisation' and the 'slow scholarship' movement discussed by Maggie Berg and Barbara Seeber in their 2016 publication, *The Slow Professor*.[6] Those who challenge the culture of speed in the academy see this as a route to restoring humanistic values to an educational system that has become degraded by managerial and commercial pressures. These concerns strongly echo those expressed by Robin Alston in 1993, who said that the growth of digital libraries may be 'a fine prospect for faculties of engineering, and the makers of electronic devices on which the librarian is increasingly dependent, but it might have serious consequences for a balanced view of who we are, where we came from, and where we are going'. Just as Alston called for librarians to develop a blend of ancient and modern outlooks, so likewise digital scholars need to be able to hold in balance slow digitisation and mass digitisation approaches.

Alston pointed out how much of our approach to digitisation has been shaped by the history of microfilm. The origins of microphotography go back to the nineteenth century, but it began to appear in commercial use in the 1920s.[7] The potential of microfilm for spreading knowledge appeared to be immense. In his book *World Brain* published in 1938, H.G. Wells noted that 'the British Museum library is making microfilms of the 4,000 books it possesses which were published before 1550',[8] and Wells anticipated that before long with the aid of microfilm 'any student, in any part of the world, will be able to sit with his projector in his own study at his or her convenience to examine *any* book, *any* docu-

---

[6]    Maggie Berg and Barbara K. Seeber, *The Slow Professor: Challenging the culture of speed in the academy* (Toronto: University of Toronto Press, 2016).

[7]    S. John Teague, *Microform, Video and Electronic Media Librarianship* (London: Butterworths, 1985), 8–9.

[8]    H.G. Wells, *World Brain* (New York: Doubleday, 1938), 76–7.

ment, in an exact replica'.[9] Wells saw microfilm libraries as a key com-
ponent in his vision of a world brain which, incorporating a constantly
updated world encyclopaedia encapsulating human knowledge, was freely
available to everyone. Wells hoped that the world brain, operated by
an enhanced global educational system, would 'replace our multitude of
unco-ordinated ganglia, our powerless miscellany of universities, research
institutions, literatures with a purpose, national educational systems and
the like'.[10]

The Library of Congress began to microfilm materials in British libraries in the early 1930s, and the British Museum became interested in the
extent to which microfilm could be used to reduce wear and tear on
fragile items in its collections.[11] In 1935, Eugene Power helped set up a
programme at the British Museum for the microfilming of rare books.
In 1938, Power established University Microfilms International at Ann
Arbor in Michigan, and launched a programme to microfilm all the
books published in English before 1700. During the Second World War,
with funding from the Rockefeller Foundation and assistance from the
American Council of Learned Societies, University Microfilms undertook
a huge programme to microfilm manuscripts and archives in danger of
loss and destruction in Britain. The microfilms produced by this British
Manuscripts Project, which are still a valuable research resource, were
catalogued at the University of Michigan Library, and sets of microfilm
were deposited in the Library of Congress.[12]

The period after the Second World War saw the large-scale deployment of microform by libraries as a means of supporting preservation.
Companies such as UMI (which became Bell and Howell in 1999 and
ProQuest in 2001),[13] Gale (founded in 1954 and now part of the Cengage
group),[14] Adam Matthew (now a subsidiary of Sage),[15] and Chadwyck-

[9]   Wells, *World Brain*, 77.
[10]  Wells, *World Brain*, xvi.
[11]  P.R. Harris, *A History of the British Museum Library, 1753–1973* (London:
The British Library, 1998), 530–1; Teague, *Microform, Video and Electronic Media
Librarianship*, 8–9.
[12]  'American Council of Learned Societies, British Manuscripts Project', *PMLA*
59, Supplement (1944), 1463–88; Lester K. Born, *British Manuscripts Project: A
checklist of the microfilms prepared in England and Wales for the American Council
of Learned Societies* (Washington, DC: Library of Congress, 1955).
[13]  https://www.proquest.com/about/history-milestones/ (accessed 20 November
2018).
[14]  https://en.wikipedia.org/wiki/Gale_(publisher) (accessed 20 November 2018).
[15]  https://en.wikipedia.org/wiki/Adam_Matthew_Digital (accessed 20 November

Healey (acquired by ProQuest in 1999),[16] produced short-run, high-cost microform publications of manuscript, archival and rare book materials that were intended for sale to a limited number of research libraries. These companies now dominate the commercial market for digital publication of primary materials. Libraries also developed collaborative projects for the microfilming of particular categories of material such as the Newsplan project for the systematic preservation of newspapers in Ireland and the United Kingdom.[17] There were also a handful of microfilming projects initiated and directed by academic communities, most notably the Anglo-Saxon Manuscripts in Microfiche Facsimile project (which now offers digital files instead of microfiche).[18]

Much of the way in which digital resources have developed is shaped by these initial experiences with microform. Many of the images in packages such as Early English Books Online, Eighteenth-Century Collections Online and the Burney Collection of Newspapers produced by former microform publishers such as Gale and ProQuest are scans from their microform publications. Even the images in some archival resources such as the online Ancient Petitions and probate copies of wills from the Prerogative Court of Canterbury produced by The National Archives are scans from microfilm. Early advocates of digital imaging such as Peter Robinson presented it chiefly as a more convenient and robust alternative to microfilm.[19] Microfilm offers the simplest imaginable view of a book or manuscript: a consecutive series of flat images offering only one fixed perspective on the volume. The reduction of manuscript pages to a single-size greyscale image strips the book of much of its distinctive identity as the book is reduced to transferable information. Looking at the original manuscript after seeing it on a microfilm reader can sometimes be a shock, as nothing in the microfilm has prepared you for the size and character of the original volume.

Given that so many of the digital resources we currently use are produced by firms that had their roots in microform publication, it is not surprising that microform precedents profoundly shape the way in which

2018).

[16]    http://www.dwyck.com/ (accessed 20 November 2018).

[17]    John Lauder, 'Partnerships in Preservation: The experience of the Newsplan 2000 Project', *IFLA Journal* 29:1 (2003), 4751.

[18]    Anglo-Saxon Manuscript in Microfiche Facsimile project (ASMMF), https://acmrs.org/publications/other/asmmf (accessed 12 November 2018).

[19]    Peter Robinson, *The Digitization of Primary Textual Materials* (Oxford: Office for Humanities Communication, 1993).

digital resources are presented. While there are, as we will see, a number of projects that offer alternative and more experimental views of how manuscripts and books can be digitally presented, for the most part the online presentation of manuscripts and other primary materials resembles colour microfilms. Much current digitisation effort has also been influenced by the example of Google Books, launched in 2002, which can in itself be seen as a resurrection of the vision of 1930s pioneers such as Wells and Power for the creation of universal global knowledge banks.[20] The launch of Google Books prompted a wave of anxiety among librarians as to how their institutions should position themselves in this new world. The way in which Google Books relied on partnerships with major research libraries brings to mind the concern expressed by Robin Alston that libraries might too easily sell out to commercial interests in pursuit of technological chimeras. The copyright difficulties and litigation encountered by Google Books, which led to a fundamental reshaping of the project, reflects another of the issues about creating knowledge hypermarkets to which Alston drew attention. Although Google Books offers the additional possibilities of keyword searching, nevertheless in many respects its vision of the structure and nature of the book is similar to that of early microfilm projects. European counterparts to Google Books, such as Europeana and Gallica,[21] although different in the way images are acquired and presented, likewise also seem to operate in the microfilm paradigm.

Digital images are easier to browse and manipulate than microfilm. We can readily magnify, rotate, crop and compare them. Moreover, colour digital images are cheaper and easier to produce than colour microfilm. We can more easily keep and share copies of digital images than microfilm. But otherwise the way in which digital images of primary textual materials are presented is often surprisingly similar to microfilm. The limitations will be familiar to anyone who regularly uses the digitised manuscripts collection on the British Library website. The current British Library manuscripts viewer (the new Universal Viewer is being rolled out for the British Library,[22] but it isn't clear how far it will improve matters) uses a Flash-based interface to restrict and control our interaction with the images. The result is very like an online microfilm viewer. You scroll

[20] The geopolitical and cultural implications of Google Books and Europeana are brilliantly analysed by Nanna Bonde Thylstrup in *The Politics of Mass Digitization* (Cambridge, MA: MIT Press, 2019).
[21] https://www.europeana.eu (accessed 12 November 2018); https://gallica.bnf.fr (accessed 12 November 2018].
[22] https://universalviewer.io/ (accessed 13 November 2018).

through the images sequentially or you can jump to a particular folio. You can view either a single page, facing pages, or the recto and verso of a folio. There are zoom controls. That's about it. The British Library and Bibliothèque Nationale de France have recently with the support of the Polonsky Foundation digitised 80 decorated manuscripts made in France and England between 700 and 1200, and a heavily curated website giving access to these manuscripts was launched in November 2018.[23] The Polonsky uses Mirador, one of the new generation of International Image Interoperability Framework (IIIF) viewers,[24] which offers more functionality in the way of comparing images from different repositories and undertaking more sophisticated image manipulation, but the precedent of the microfilm reader still looms large – the view options in Mirador offer a choice between a scroll view, which is like microfilm, a gallery view, which recalls microfiche and an image view, which combines both.

For Eugene Power and the early pioneers of microfilm, the aim was to undertake a one-off transfer of the information in books and manuscripts from one medium to another. Likewise, digitisation is currently often seen as a once and for all process. We talk of manuscripts being 'digitised' as if one set of shots is the beginning and end of the matter. However, we can be certain that it will before too long be necessary to take further digital images of the manuscripts covered by the Polonsky project. Camera quality will improve, and it will be possible to take higher-resolution images that show more detail. New techniques such as multi-spectral imaging or reflectance transformation imaging (RTI) offer the potential for fresh insights into the manuscript. We may want to use X-ray or CT imaging to examine under drawing in decorations. For the truly committed scholar seeking to understand the history of a manuscript or book, a single view will never be enough. A scholar exploring a manuscript may want to compare images of the manuscript made in 1940 with those from 1990 and 2010. Scholars wish to explore manuscripts from every different perspective. Digital images offer that possibility, if we use them imaginatively enough.

The pressures that drive mass digitisation are very similar to those underpinning the growth of the managerial audit culture in universities to which the slow scholarship movement is a reaction. Librarians and curators are encouraged to increase access and the number of people who engage with their collections. The number of items digitised and the number of

---

[23]    https://manuscrits-france-angleterre.org/ (accessed 21 November 2018).
[24]    https://projectmirador.org (accessed 12 November 2018).

hits received by each item are key performance indicators for many libraries, archives and museums. Documents like the British Library's annual report highlight the millions of pages digitised, and declare that 'every day, the Library's physical and digital spaces are teeming with people working to advance knowledge',[25] but it is unclear how the 25 million visits to the British Library's website during 2017–18 contributed to the advancement of knowledge.[26] Nevertheless, the Library's KPI targets for 2017–18 included such figures as 4 million website items consulted, 160,000 digital items acquired through legal deposit, and 6 million visitors to the British Library Learning website.[27] The emphasis throughout is on scale and large numbers, regardless of quality and with little regard for how such activities really advance knowledge.

In Britain, a pernicious expression of government and institutional pressure on libraries and archives to increase access through digitisation as quickly as possible has been the use of commercial partnerships to undertake digitisation projects, a cultural counterpart to the discredited Private Finance Initiative. The baleful effects of this are illustrated by the digitisation of newspapers. The Burney Collection of eighteenth-century newspapers held by the British Library, the largest and most important collection of eighteenth-century newspapers, was digitised by Gale Cengage.[28] The Burney Collection has been licensed by JISC Collections for use by UK universities, and is widely available to UK researchers. However, the second most important collection of early newspapers, the Nichols Collection in the Bodleian Library, was digitised by Adam Mathew, and this digital package is less widely available. Gale has recently produced its own version of the Nichols Collection, but this does not currently seem to have been acquired by many libraries. Indeed, if you want to consult the Nichols Collection digitally, the best thing to do is to go to the Bodleian Library, which seems to miss the whole point of digitisation.

This would be annoying enough, but in order to meet deadlines for the sale and disposal of its Newspaper Library at Colindale, the British Library arranged for the remainder of its newspapers to be digitised by

---

[25]   *British Library Annual Report and Accounts 2017–18* (London: The British Library, 2018), HC 1255, 6.

[26]   *British Library Annual Report 2017–18*, 37.

[27]   *British Library Annual Report 2017–18*, 36–7.

[28]   Andrew Prescott, 'Searching for Dr Johnson: The digitisation of the Burney Newspaper Collection', in *Travelling Chronicles: News and newspapers from the early modern period to the eighteenth century*, ed. S.G. Brandtzæg, P. Goring and C. Watson (Leiden: Brill, 2018), 49–71.

the family history firm Findmypast. As a result, access to the British Newspaper Archive requires an individual subscription of at least £85 a year (depending on which package you choose).[29] Library subscriptions do not appear to be available, and few university libraries offer access to the British Newspaper Archive. There is free access if you go to the British Library itself, but again this seems to run counter to the very concept of digitisation enhancing access. Two decades of extensive effort and investment in digitisation has indeed enhanced the availability of newspapers, but the haste to digitise has produced a fragmented and confusing landscape. Curiously, the microfilm approach to newspapers was far more structured. The microfilm edition of eighteenth-century newspapers attempted to provide integrated runs of titles from the Burney and Nichols collections,[30] while Newsplan achieved systematic microfilm of nineteenth-century material. The fragmented digital coverage of UK newspapers recalls the words of Robin Alston in 1993:

> It seems to me an irony that would not have escaped Swift that at precisely the point in time when scholarship has begun to accept the principle of the unity of knowledge and the value of interdisciplinary research we are bent upon its fragmentation.

The pressure to maximise digital coverage has led many archives to rely on family history firms to digitise as much material as possible, with little regard for how the digital record is then made available. The most popular activity on the web after pornography is family history research,[31] and there is big money involved. The British Library holds the India Office Records, which include many of the genealogical records for India during British rule. In order to get these records digitised as quickly as possible, the British Library struck a deal with the family history website Findmypast.[32] Findmypast digitised the records, but if you want to

---

[29]   https://www.britishnewspaperarchive.co.uk/account/subscribe (accessed 13 November 2018).
[30]   http://microformguides.gale.com/Data/Introductions/10030FM.htm (accessed 20 November 2018).
[31]   Bruce Falconer, 'Ancestry.com's Genealogical Juggernaut', *Businessweek*, 20 September 2012, http://www.businessweek.com/articles/2012-09-20/ancestry-dot-coms-genealogical-juggernaut (accessed 13 February 2014); Gregory Rodriguez, 'How Genealogy Became Almost as Popular as Porn', *Time*, 30 May 2014, http://time.com/133811/how-genealogy-became-almost-as-popular-as-porn/ (accessed 12 November 2018).
[32]   'Hidden History of the British in India', British Library press release, 29

consult the records outside the British Library, you need a subscription to Findmypast, which can cost as much as £156 a year.[33] These records are not generally available in university libraries. Under pressure to digitise as much as possible, many archives have made agreements allowing firms like Ancestry and Findmypast to digitise key records such as the census, parish registers and rate books. In order to access these records you need subscriptions to these companies. You also have to grapple with interfaces that are aimed at amateur family historians and are unsuited for complex queries. This is nothing less than the privatisation by stealth of our historical heritage in order to fulfil arbitrary management targets to demonstrate increased use and access.

We need alternative models of digital engagement. We need urgently to think beyond the commercial microform precedent in shaping our digital resources. I cut my digital teeth working with Kevin Kiernan on the *Electronic Beowulf* project in the 1990s. *Electronic Beowulf* was one of the first digital editions produced under the auspices of the British Library and includes a complete colour facsimile of Cotton MS Vitellius A.xv, which contains the only known medieval text of *Beowulf*.[34] The British Library has since digitised Cotton MS Vitellius A.xv anew at a much higher resolution, and these images are available on the British Library website.[35] It might therefore be assumed that *Electronic Beowulf* has been superseded by the new digital facsimile on the British Library site, but this is far from the case. As a result of the fire damage to the manuscript in 1731, many readings in the manuscript can only be made out under ultra-violet light. This has been known for many years, and in the black-and-white facsimile of the Nowell Codex edited by Kemp Malone and published in *Early English Manuscripts in Facsimile* in 1963,[36] the British Museum photographer reproduced some pages

January 2014, https://www.bl.uk/press-releases/2014/january/hidden-history-of-the-british-in-india (accessed 14 November 2018).

[33] Rosemary Collins, 'Findmypast introduces new pricing structure', *Who Do You Think You Are?*, 27 November 2017, http://www.whodoyouthinkyo-uaremagazine.com/news/findmypast-introduces-new-pricing-structure (accessed 14 November 2018).

[34] http://ebeowulf.uky.edu (accessed 13 November 2018). For information about the history of the project, see http://www.uky.edu/~kiernan/eBeo_archives/ (accessed 14 November 2018).

[35] http://www.bl.uk/manuscripts/FullDisplay.aspx?index=4&ref=Cotton_MS_Vitellius_A_XV (accessed 13 November 2018).

[36] Kemp Malone (ed.), *The Nowell Codex: British Museum Cotton Vitellius A. XV, second MS.* Early English Manuscripts in Facsimile 12 (Copenhagen: Rosenkilde

under ultra-violet light. The digital version on the British Library's dig-itised manuscripts website does not include any imaging under ultra-violet light. As a result, readings that are visible in the black-and-white photographic facsimile cannot be seen in the colour digital images on the British Library's own website. On the other hand, the imaging of readings under special lighting conditions was a particular focus of *Electronic Beowulf*, which provides comprehensive pictorial coverage of such readings. In short, anyone engaged in serious work on the *Beowulf* manuscript should always use the older *Electronic Beowulf* rather than the more recent defective British Library version.

The fact that the British Library's library of digitised manuscripts can include a facsimile of the Nowell Codex that is less useful for research purposes than the 1963 black-and-white facsimile illustrates the dangers of a one-size-fits-all production-line approach to the digitisation of manuscripts. By contrast, *Electronic Beowulf* epitomises the virtues and potential of a slow digitisation approach. This is because it was driven by the scholarly vision and profound knowledge of the manuscript of its editor Kevin Kiernan, rather than deriving from a more mechanis-tic digitisation programme. *Electronic Beowulf* provides high-resolution colour images of Cotton MS Vitellius A.xv in its entirety, but it goes much further than this. All readings under ultra-violet light are imaged and documented. Moreover, the hundreds of letters in the manuscript concealed under paper frames when the manuscript was conserved in the nineteenth century were imaged using fibre-optic backlighting, some-thing that had not been possible until digital cameras were available. In this way, a mass of new information about the *Beowulf* text was recovered and documented.

This intensive forensic imaging of Cotton MS Vitellius A.xv is accompanied in *Electronic Beowulf* by an extensive image archive of primary materials relating to the transmission of the *Beowulf* text. Users can compare readings in the manuscript with both sets of transcripts made in the eighteenth century for the Danish antiquary Thorkelin, and with the detailed collations of Thorkelin's edition made by Sir Frederic Madden and John Conybeare, offering a comprehensive archive of information about readings in the manuscript prior to its conservation in 1845. *Electronic Beowulf* is far from being the sort of do-it-yourself edition that Robin Alston feared, however. It is accompanied by a tran-script and full edition by Kevin Kiernan that incorporates sophisticated

& Bagger, 1963).

searching and options allowing metrical, grammatical and other aspects of the text to be readily explored.

In the way in which *Electronic Beowulf* uses imaging to open up the various layers of evidence within the manuscript and facilitates comparison with other relevant materials, *Electronic Beowulf* fulfils the vision of slow digitisation that Lorna Hughes and I outlined in our *Archive Journal* article:

> 'Slow digitisation' would gradually explore the different layers of evidence in a manuscript, just as an archaeologist might very slowly and carefully examine a pot. Rather than creating one single digital representation of a manuscript to support 'access,' the use of a variety of digital tools to gradually explore a manuscript in-depth can generate an archive of information about one single manuscript that, as well as supporting scholarship, also provides a much deeper educational experience.[37]

Whereas the simplistic representation of Cotton MS Vitellius A.xv on the British Library's digitised manuscript site conceals vital evidence about the manuscript and misleads the viewer into thinking the *Beowulf* text is simpler than it is, *Electronic Beowulf* confronts the user at every point with the complexity and difficulty of the manuscript evidence for *Beowulf*. Reminding us how complex, deceptive and bewildering manuscripts can be should surely be one of the functions of digitisation. But it isn't a process that can be done simply and quickly. Creating elaborate digital archives like *Electronic Beowulf* is an expensive, time-consuming and above all slow business. It is slower and more intellectually taxing than writing articles and books. It requires a large team of collaborators and many different resources. It won't fit easily in research assessment timetables. But ultimately it will help generate more profound knowledge about the manuscript than a series of quick snapshots. This is slow scholarship, on the side of the ancients, but it is surely what humanities scholars should be doing.

It may seem that the *Electronic Beowulf* is an unusual example, because the damage to the manuscript in 1731 means that use of special lighting and other techniques is essential in imaging the manuscript. But of course many other Cotton manuscripts were also damaged in 1731, and the use of the approaches pioneered in *Electronic Beowulf* will yield dividends in investigating these manuscripts as well. A.S.G. Edwards has recently criticised the British Library for failing to use digital methods to examine the

---

[37] Prescott and Hughes, 'Why Do We Digitise'?

burnt Cotton manuscripts.[38] Edwards doesn't mention *Electronic Beowulf*, but nevertheless the potential of these methods to further the process of exploring the burnt Cotton manuscripts is immense. It is consequently baffling that the British Library, in pursuit of fulfilling KPIs by maximising the number of items digitised, persists in adding to its site images of manuscripts badly damaged in 1731 that cry out for the kind of special treatment developed by *Electronic Beowulf* project. Kevin Kiernan demonstrated in the *Electronic Boethius* project how much can be recovered from the Alfredian translation of the *Consolation of Philosophy* in Cotton MS. Otho A.vi by the use of ultra-violet light and imaging processing.[39] This makes it bizarre that the British Library only shows plain light images of Otho A.vi on its digitised images website. Similarly, the Gildas manuscript, Cotton MS. Vitellius A.vi, has many badly damaged folios that would benefit from multi-spectral imaging, but again the British Library only offers plain light images. The use of backlighting to reveal sections of the manuscript concealed by paper frames is also a technique that has enormous potential to recover letters and words concealed since the nineteenth century in many Cotton manuscripts, but there is no sign of the British Library experimenting with such techniques. Although the British Library has developed great expertise in multi-spectral imaging, there does not appear to be any systematic programme for its use. Multi-spectral imaging of very badly burnt manuscripts such as Cotton MS Otho B.x, an early eleventh-century collection of mostly saints' lives by the monk Ælfric (but currently undescribed in the British Library catalogue), has enormous potential for recovery of hitherto unstudied texts, as Kevin Kiernan demonstrated twenty-five years ago.[40]

There are many other exemplars of slow digitisation. Bill Endres's remarkable work on the St Chad Gospels not only provides spellbinding

---

[38]   A.S.G. Edwards, 'The Digital Archive, Scholarly Enquiry, and the Study of Medieval English Manuscripts', *Archive Journal*, September 2018, http://www.archivejournal.net/essays/digital-archive-scholarly-enquiry-and-the-study-of-medieval-english-manuscripts/ (accessed 15 November 2018).

[39]   Kevin Kiernan, 'Alfred the Great's Burnt Boethius', in *The Iconic Page in Manuscript, Print and Digital Culture*, ed. G. Bornstein and T. Tinkle (Ann Arbor, MI: University of Michigan Press: 1998), 7–32; Kevin Kiernan et al., 'The ARCHway Project: Architecture for Research in Computing for Humanities through research, teaching, and learning', *Literary and Linguistic Computing* 20 (2005), 69–88; Susan Irvine, 'Fragments of Boethius: The reconstruction of the Cotton manuscript of the Alfredian text', *Anglo-Saxon England* 34 (2005), 169–81.

[40]   Kevin Kiernan, 'British Library MS Cotton Otho B. x, fol. 13(54v)r', http://www.uky.edu/~kiernan/eBeo_archives/OBx/ (accessed 13 November 2018).

images of a beautiful insular manuscript, but the range of imaging techniques used by Bill provides many varied perspectives on the manuscript.[41] The 3D images of the Chad Gospels can help anticipate where conservation issues might arise in the manuscript. Bill has developed an archive of images of the Chad Gospels that allow issues like pigment deterioration to be pinpointed. The Chad Gospels project provides comprehensive coverage of views of the manuscript under different light wavelengths. While the British Library seems more concerned in its digitised manuscripts website with maximising coverage, it has nevertheless hosted some good examples of slow digitisation methods, such as its digital version of the early Biblical manuscript, Codex Sinaiticus.[42] The digital Codex Sinaiticus reunites parts of the manuscript currently split between London, St Petersburg, Leipzig and Mount Sinai. As well as images under standard light, it also provides images under raking light, enabling ruling, erasures and other information to be easily made out. The images are accompanied by a transcription in Greek and English translation. The digital Codex Sinaiticus invites us to explore the complexities of the manuscript rather than providing a flat single-dimensional view of it.

Slow digitisation is not necessarily restricted to projects using special lighting and imaging techniques. Another standard bearer for slow digitisation at the British Library is the International Dunhuang Project.[43] The Buddhist cave library near the city of Dunhuang on the edge of the Gobi Desert contained approximately 40,000 manuscripts, paintings and printed documents documenting the rich culture of life on the Silk Road between 100 BCE and 1000 CE. This cave was sealed up at the end of the first millennium and only rediscovered by archaeologists in 1900. The contents of the cave library, however, were dispersed across many institutions throughout the world, making it difficult to understand the nature and context of the library. The International Dunhuang Project is a vast undertaking that seeks to digitally reintegrate the Dunhuang cave library and add to it tens of thousands of other artefacts discovered by archaeologists in Silk Road cities at the beginning of the twentieth century. The International Dunhuang Project is a large-scale digitisation project embracing many international partners whose database currently contains over 522,000 images. But the project is driven by the vision of slowly and meticulously reuniting these huge dispersed collections. It is motivated by the scholarly need to understand the context and

---

41   https://lichfield.ou.edu/ (accessed 19 November 2018).
42   https://www.codexsinaiticus.org (accessed 19 November 2018).
43   https://idp.bl.uk (accessed 19 November 2018).

structure of these collections. It has over a period of twenty-five years sought to enhance our understanding of these documents in ways that would not otherwise be possible. In these ways, it epitomises the values of slow digitisation.

Slow digitisation is just as relevant to modern records as to ancient and medieval manuscripts. When David Livingstone was stuck in the Congolese village of Bambarre for nearly seven months between 1870 and 1871, he ran low on supplies, and ran out of ink and paper. Using scraps of a newspaper and old letters, however, Livingstone was able to keep writing his field diary using local African dye made from plants. These manuscripts were deposited in the National Library of Scotland, but the dye-ink faded and the diaries could not be read with the naked eye. However, the David Livingstone Spectral Imaging project, directed by Professor Adrian Wisnicki of Indiana University of Pennsylvania and Birkbeck, University of London, used multi-spectral imaging to retrieve Livingstone's text and prepare an edition of his 1871 field diary.[44]

An illustration of the potential of slow digitisation approaches for early modern records is the *Signed, Sealed and Undelivered* project involving collaborators from MIT, Utrecht University, Leiden University, University of Groningen, University of Oxford, Queen Mary University of London and King's College London.[45] The postmasters of the Dutch city of The Hague at the end of the seventeenth century, Simon de Brienne and his wife Maria Germain, were at the centre of European communication networks at the time when William of Orange was seizing the British throne. The Briennes left behind a trunk containing 2,600 unopened letters. Using the latest advances in X-ray imaging from the field of dentistry developed by David Mills and the Apocalypto group at Queen Mary University of London, the project is reading and editing these sealed letters without opening them, which would destroy important evidence on letter-writing practice.

Manuscripts and books of all types and periods constantly reveal new secrets and surprises when interrogated in this way. A slow digitisation approach assumes there is always something fresh to discover in a manuscript, no matter how well known it is and how often it has been imaged. A good illustration of this is the hyperspectral imaging by the Library of Congress of Thomas Jefferson's draft of the Declaration of Independence, which revealed how Jefferson changed the word 'subjects' to 'citizens'.[46]

[44]  https://livingstone.library.ucla.edu (accessed 19 November 2018).
[45]  https://brienne.org.
[46]  'Hyperspectral Imaging by Library of Congress Reveals Change Made by

Multi-spectral imaging has also been used recently to study the writing process of Jorge Luis Borges.[47]

But slow digitisation is expensive, time-consuming and demanding in resources. *Electronic Beowulf* required the collaboration of academics, conservators, curators, photographers and computer scientists. In many ways one of the most exciting outcomes of *Electronic Beowulf* was the way in which it enabled these different groups to discuss and debate the digitisation process rather than (as is too often the case now) simply accept what large institutions like the British Library are willing to provide. In the early days of digitisation, it seemed that one of the great potential benefits of digitisation would be that collaborative projects like *Electronic Beowulf* would promote greater dialogue and shared working between libraries and archives and academic researchers. It was hoped that this might create new disciplinary and research configurations. However, this has not happened to the extent that might have been anticipated. Libraries have happily reverted to offering 'users' set patterns of service and digital provision on something of a take-it-or-leave-it basis. Academics are often puzzled as to how to build a dialogue. Managerially, of course, this is a much less demanding approach, but does it promote the shared creation of knowledge? We might hope that 'slow digitisation' might break down such barriers.

It is understandable that librarians, under political pressure to increase use of and access to their collections, jib at the cost of what has been called 'boutique digitisation', but this is perhaps partly because of ways in which the arguments for digitisation have been expressed. Major libraries take great pride in the slow and costly processes by which rare books and manuscripts are conserved, and see this as part of a necessary investment in our shared cultural heritage. Perhaps we should also view the slow and meticulous digitisation of manuscripts like *Beowulf*, which add immeasurably to our understanding of these cultural monuments, in a similar way.

The contemporary battle of the books is part of a war of resistance against audit, efficiency, key performance indicators, management lifecycles and workload models. It is a battle to protect the books from being

---

Thomas Jefferson in Original Declaration of Independence Draft', Library of Congress press release, 2 July 2010, https://www.loc.gov/item/prn-10-161/analysis-reveals-changes-in-declaration-of-independence/2010-07-02/ (accessed 19 November 2010).

[47] Nora Benedict, 'Digital Approaches to the Archive: Multispectral imaging and the recovery of Borges's writing process in "El muerto" and "La casa de Asterión"', *Variaciones Borges* 45 (2018), 153–69.

overwhelmed by the amorphous idea of information. Our battle resists information. At the heart of computational thinking is Claude Shannon's information theory, which sees a distinction between the message, comprising data consisting of bits, and the medium carrying the message. This idea is embedded in much editorial theory in the humanities and is fundamental to such key aspects of digital humanities as the Text Encoding Initiative. Yet we cannot disentangle the history of a poem such as *Beowulf* from the manuscript in which it is preserved. Our understanding of a complex poem such as *Piers Plowman* depends fundamentally on our understanding of the many manuscripts in which it is preserved. For the humanities, the medium and the information are profoundly and inescapably intertwined. Much of what we study in the humanities is the history and result of that interaction. By assuming that the information in a book can be separated from its physical context and transferred to a new medium, we risk losing all understanding of the nature of the book. Books and manuscripts are not information.

Slow digitisation resists assumptions about the priority of information and seeks to enlist digital tools in a more dynamic and pro-active engagement with books and manuscripts as artefacts. Of course, there is a place for mass digitisation approaches, but we should not assume that this is the only approach. 'One size fits all' is never a helpful approach in humanities scholarship. Beside the mass digitisation programmes, it is vital that there is also space for the more experimental probing and investigation that is at the heart of slow digitisation. Books and manuscripts are after all craft productions, and by likewise using digital methods in a craft manner, rather than using production- line methods, we will enhance our understanding of the way in which books and manuscripts were created. By using craft methods of digitisation, we will develop a fuller and more rounded understanding of the objects we digitise. The battle of the books is one that defends a view of books, manuscripts and archives as complex artefacts not as carriers of information. Slow digitisation is an ideology of resistance against superficial views of information and, as Robin Alston first reminded us, at stake in this battle is the survival of the books themselves.

# Index